— The —
Establishing Grace
or
Holiness in the Book of Romans

— By —

A. M. Hills, D. D.

Author of
Holiness and Power
The Uttermost Salvation
Fundamental Christian Theology
etc., etc.

ISBN 0-88019-187-2

 Schmul Publishing Co., Inc.
Wesleyan Book Club   Salem, Ohio
1990

INTRODUCTION

Dr. Hills is conceded to be in the very foremost rank of theologians in the holiness movement. This short treatise is as fine a piece of work as Dr. Hills ever has done and we feel that it should be given a wide circulation.

The doctrine of entire sanctification as set forth in the New Testament, and as advocated by the Wesleyan movement, has been the subject of much misunderstanding and prejudice. But could it be proved that sin must remain in the heart of a believer during the course of his natural life, even the most serious objection that could be raised against it would be that those who advocate it maintain too high an estimate of the redemptive power of the blood of Christ and too exalted an ideal of Christianity.

But the author reviews the entire sin question in the light of the fullness of the New Testament dispensation and shows conclusively from the scriptures that the atoning work of Jesus Christ must forever have as its objective, the deliverance from all sin and the infilling and indwelling of the Holy Spirit as an abiding Comforter.

H. ORTON WILEY, *President, Pasadena College.*

CONTENTS

The Establishing Grace

CHAPTER I

SANCTIFICATION THE ESTABLISHING GRACE

"Therefore being justified by faith, we have peace with God through our Lord Jesus Christ: through whom also we have had our access (by faith) into this grace wherein we stand, and we rejoice in hope of the glory of God" (Rom. 5:1, 2).

This is the beginning of one of the most difficult passages in the Bible to interpret. It has been for centuries the battle-ground of theologians. But its purpose is plain. It is designed to exhibit the benefits of the gospel plan of salvation. The apostle has fully established in the preceding chapters:

1. That men were under condemnation for sin;
2. That this involved alike both Jews and Gentiles;
3. That there was no escape now for any but by pardon, not by merit but by grace;
4. That this plan was fully made known by the gospel of Christ; and
5. That this is no new doctrine, but was the way in which both Abraham and David had been accepted before God.

Thus we have here the shining way set forth, that leads from the gross darkness of heathenism in the first chapter to the glorious life of holiness depicted in the twelfth chapter.

There are two blessings named in the text. The first verse sets forth the one: the second verse begins the description of the other. The first is called "Justification by Faith": the second is called "Sanctification by Faith." We cannot change the *order* of these blessings. The second cannot come first to the heart. Nor are they simultaneous. There are necessary and essential reasons why they are successive experiences. The first is for repentant sinners; the second is only for the sons of God.

So He always pleads with sinners to repent and be pardoned: but He is always solicitous for Christians that they should be sanctified.

We will therefore discuss the texts in the natural and divine order.

I. Consider the First Blessing—

JUSTIFICATION BY FAITH

This is the truth of the Reformation, the great foundation principle of Protestantism, the blessed hope of a fallen world. No more tyranny of priesthoods now. No more prescribed ceremonials. No more penances, and pilgrimages to shrines, or sacrifices of vain oblations, or useless works to merit salvation. "Not by works of righteousness which we have done, but by His mercy He saved us through the washing of regeneration, and renewing of the Holy Spirit, which He poured out upon us richly, through Jesus Christ our Savior, that being *justified by His grace,* we might be made heirs according to the hope of eternal life."

Jesus took our place, honored the government we had dishonored, obeyed the law that we had broken. As a governmental expedient, He, the Governor of the universe Himself, suffered vicariously as we deserved to suffer, and now He can be just and yet offer salvation on proper terms to all offenders. This He freely does. He takes a solemn oath before the universe that He has no pleasure in the death of the wicked, and that it is not His will that any should perish. He longs to save all, and the atonement He has made makes it now proper and possible for Him, consistently with the interests of His government, and His own honor, and the well-being of all His subjects, to save all who will comply with the simple conditions of salvation.

1. AND THESE CONDITIONS ARE FULLY AND PLAINLY MADE KNOWN. They are as follows:

(1) *Negatively.* Not by any rite or ceremony, as baptism, or partaking of the Sacrament, or by confirmation, or going to the church, or joining it, or by reading the Bible, or by cultivating morality or by self-reformation. Any or all of these may be good in their place, but none of them is a condition of salvation, and all of them together cannot bring it about.

(2) *Positively.* The conditions are:

(a) *Repentance of sin.* Sin has been the cause of all the trouble in the moral universe. It is a wilful rebellion against God. It is an assault upon His holiness and the character of His government. It is a revolt against the authority of the Most High. It is a wanton attempt to subvert and defeat all the holy purposes of God for the good of moral beings. As such, sin must be fully confessed and heartily forsaken. This is the primal condition of any peace with God. All the forces of the divine government must be forever arrayed against that malignant evil that is destroying the happiness of the beings He loves and created for His glory. Repentance means to abhor, and confess, and renounce all sin, as the first step toward reconciliation, the first condition of abiding peace.

(*b*) The other essential condition is *faith*. And that faith is not merely, as some suppose, a mere intellectual assent to doctrine, or a mental apprehension of truth. The action of all the faculties of the moral nature is involved. Faith is that belief of the intellect, that consent of the affections, and that act of the will by which the soul commits itself to Christ Jesus for salvation. Saving faith apprehends the atoning work of Christ as the divine remedy for sin, trusts directly therein, and receives forgiveness as the immediate gift of God.

2. Notice the Results

(1) *"We are justified,"* says the text. Justification is that judicial act of God by which, on condition of the sinner's repentance of sin and faith in the atoning Saviour, He pardons his sins, remits the penalty, restores him to the divine favor, and treats him as if he had never sinned.

(2) *"We have peace with God's law and government."* We have now consented to them, and admitted that they were always righteous. We have fallen in with God's plan of reconciliation, and His indignation is no longer kindled against us. No more do thunderbolts of divine wrath hang over us. Hell no longer yawns for our advancing feet. The divine government recognizes us now as the sons of God. We have received the divine life into our souls, and are born again into the family of God.

(3) *This settles the sin-question.* Sin had to be forsaken to get this blessing of sonship, and it costs as much to keep the blessing as it did to get it. "We know that whosoever is begotten of God sinneth not." When pro-

fessors of religion sport with sin, they are backslidden and have lost their experience.

II. Notice the blessing of the second verse.

"Through whom also." "Also" means something in addition. There is, in other words, a second epochal experience, after regeneration, which God has for the soul, and invites us all to obtain, in this epistle. It is called in the next chapter "sanctification." It is described as being "free from the sin." The Century Dictionary defines sanctification as "The act of God's grace by which the affections of men are purified, and the soul is cleansed from sin," bringing "conformity of heart and life to the will of God." The Standard Dictionary defines it as "The gracious work of the Holy Spirit whereby *the believer* is freed from sin, and exalted to holiness of heart and life." Notice, it is only the *"believer"*—the man already a Christian—who can receive this blessing: and it is wrought "by the Holy Spirit."

1. NOTICE THAT IT IS DESCRIBED IN THIS VERSE AS "THE GRACE WHEREIN WE STAND." It has been well called "the standing grace," for it makes it easier to keep our religious experience, and "to stand" against the wiles of the devil, and not "fall" or "backslide." And this is most manifestly true, because:

(1) *It removes abnormal physical appetites.* I have heard literally thousands testify to having lost their appetites for tobacco and intoxicants and drugs, and the passion for gambling, in a moment of time.

(2) *It removes the abnormal out of the natural appetites* that are in themselves perfectly innocent, and are divinely provided as essential to our very being. It is then easier to make them submissive to reason.

(3) *It cleanses from the depraved propensity to sin,* the disordered condition of all our sensibilities that produces a sad proclivity to evil. When this is accomplished by sanctifying grace, temptations are no longer internal, but external, and have less power over the soul. The proneness to wander from God is displaced by a sweet attraction for God. The heart is spoiled for the world, and finds a charm in heavenly things. For all these and many more reasons to be given, it is easier to "stand" in sanctification than in the justified experience.

2. IT IS FURTHER DESCRIBED AS THE "JOY-GIVING" GRACE. "We also rejoice in our tribulations." Few unsanctified Christians ever do that. The carnal mind frets and chafes and complains under trials. It naturally murmurs under afflictions, and questions the wisdom of God's providences and the allotments of His grace. But the sanctified heart, cleansed from the spirit of repining, and fortified by a larger faith, sings in the prison of tribulation, knowing that a divine purpose planned it and that all is well.

People are scared away from this second blessing by the notion that it will rob them of all their joys. But it only weans them from the hollow and deceptive pleasures of the world, while it satisfies them with the perennial joys of heaven. They exchange the unrewarded and cruel tasks of Egypt for the love-service of Canaan: they trade leeks and garlics for Eshcol clusters; they yield up the insipid waters of the Nile, and gain the springs and streams of the Promised Land and the bountiful rains from heaven; they surrender barrenness and receive fruitfulness; they lose the drudgery of legal service and are rewarded with the gladness of pleasing God.

3. IT IS DESCRIBED AS AN EXPERIENCE OF "HOPE AND LOVE." "Tribulation worketh patience (constancy); and patience, probation (approved character—*Lange*); and approval, hope; and hope maketh not ashamed, because the love of God hath been shed abroad in our hearts through the Holy Ghost, who was given unto us." Here is the glorious fruition of this blessed second work of grace. Joyless, despondent Christians are not fair samples of what God can make of sinful men. We may have an unclouded hope, confirmed by God's own testimony shed abroad in our hearts by the incoming, sanctifying Holy Ghost—the testimony of a consciousness of God's love for us, awakening in us a reciprocal love for God. This is the holy life of perfect love which the gospel requires and makes provision for in our experience.

An illustration will be in place here. Mrs. Jonathan Edwards received the Holy Spirit baptism in 1742, and she writes: "I cannot find language to express how certain the everlasting love of God appeared; the everlasting mountains and hills were but shadows to it. My safety, and happiness, and eternal enjoyment of God's immutable love seemed as durable and unchangeable as God himself. Melted and overcome by the sweetness of this assurance, I fell into a great flow of tears, and could not forbear weeping aloud. The presence of God was so near and real that I seemed scarcely conscious of anything else. At night my soul seemed to be filled with an inexpressibly sweet and pure love to God and to the children of God, with a refreshing consolation and solace of soul which made me willing to lie on the earth at the feet of the servants of God, to declare His gracious dealings with me, and breathe forth before them my gratitude and love and praise. All night I continued in a constant, clear, and lively sense of the heavenly sweetness of Christ's excellent and transcendent love, and of His nearness to me and of my dearness to Him, with an inexpressibly sweet calmness of soul in an entire rest in Him." The above is this passage of Scripture in actual experience.

CHAPTER II

The fifth chapter of Romans mentions five times the "much more" salvation that comes to fallen man from an atoning Savior. Rom. 5:12-21 is regarded as the most difficult passage in the New Testament. It has been made needlessly difficult by the preconceived notions and theological opinions that people have read into the passage to make it support their views. May God keep us from doing this, and lead us into the truth.

At the outset we would call attention to the striking fact, as it seems to us that the Greek noun for sin (*Hamartia*) is found thirty-six times between Rom. 5:12 and Rom. 8:10, and in twenty-nine of these times it has the definite article, "the" before it, and is always in the singular number. We cannot help believing that the expression, "the sin," "the sin," so often repeated, means a particular kind of sin, namely, "indwelling sin," "inherited sin," "the sin-principle," "depravity." In several of the other seven times, when it has no article, it manifestly means actual sin.

We are the more convinced of this because over and over again it is personified as an abiding state, as a reigning queen, as a phantom man, as a slave driver or master, as a murderer, as a body of corruption, as a ruling tendency. Now it would be unnatural and unlikely to personify a sinful act, existing but an instant and then done with. It would be natural and quite probable that, if the apostle were discussing the effect of the abiding PRINCIPLE OF

15

SIN in an individual or in humanity, he would personify it, precisely as he has done. The definitions of the word in a Greek lexicon give this double meaning. The first set of definitions is—"error, offence, sin." The second set is —"*a principle or cause of sin, proneness to sin, sinful propensity.*" Manifestly, it is "the principle of sin" that the apostle is referring to where the definite article is used.

Bearing this fact in mind will throw much light on these four wonderful chapters in Romans.

1. Because it makes Paul's argument more lucid.
2. Because it brushes away, as so many theological fictions, the cobweb theories that a perverted theology has spun from these verses.
3. Because SANCTIFICATION, so often referred to, and actually named in these chapters, means the destruction of this sin-principle, the cleansing of the nature from this inherited depravity.
4. Because it is exactly this *proneness to sin,* inherited from Adam, which makes the awful conflict with right reason or conscience, aroused and illuminated by the Holy Spirit and the law of God, so vividly described by the apostle. It is precisely from this internal strife, this civil war in the breast, that the sanctifying Christ and the Holy Spirit deliver us.

VERSE 12. "Therefore, as through one man *the sin* [principle] entered into the world, and the death [principle] through *the sin* [principle]; and so death passed unto all men, for that all sinned."

Says Dr. Whedon in his Commentary: "By *the sin,* many understand the state of sin (sometimes called corruption) into which man has fallen as a nature. And no doubt there is a *state* of evil as well as evil *action,* which in the Scriptures is called *sin*. Sin is not in action alone: there may be a *permanently* wrong and *wicked state of mind*." Dean Alford says: "The kind of sin spoken of in this whole passage is both *original and actual*." Godet: "The apostle is speaking of the *principle of revolt* whereby the human will rises against the divine in all its different forms and manifestations." He again calls it "The corrupt inward disposition." "The definite article," says Lange, "before *hamartia* and also before *thanatos* denotes sin and death as a power or principle which controls man, and reveals itself in hereditary corruption and in every form of actual sin." Sin is personified as a fearful tyrant who acquired universal dominion over the human race; he "reigns in death," ver. 21; "works death in us," 7:13; "lords it over us," 6:14; "works all manner of lust," 7:8; "deceives and slays the sinner," 7:11.

Augustine and Calvin make it mean "original sin or natural depravity." Koppe, Olshausen, Webster, and Wilkinson say it means "Sinfulness; sinfulness personified; a sinful disposition."

With such ample endorsement in the world of scholarship we are sure of our ground, and we shall see exactly what Jesus undertakes to do for us, and what sanctifying grace can effect in the life.

According to the Bible, Adam's immortality was supernatural. Just so, his holiness was supernatural, "being superinduced by the blessed indwelling and communion of the Divine Spirit." Sin drove the Spirit from him, and introduced "the sin-principle"; and "the sin-principle" introduced "the death-principle" which, by the law of heredity and propagation, became a race inheritance and a race calamity. Adam's act of disobedience deranged his moral constitution. God, law, conscience, reason, were no longer supreme. Self, submission to temptation, proneness to indulge the sensibilities against the protest of the reason, took the ascendant. That changed condition of soul brought the loss of the Spirit and the incoming of "the death principle." Being hereditary, it has passed on from generation to generation. Whatever may be the suitableness of the term, "original sin," Scripture, consciousness and experience attest the mournful fact of man's depraved state, corrupt nature, and consequent subjection to death.

Here we meet a number of theological speculations: (1) "Death" here is said to mean physical, spiritual and eternal death. (2) It is further declared to be a penalty inflicted upon each member of the race of Adam. (3) But, say some theologians, there could have been no such penalty without personal guilt and fault. (4) Therefore, we were all in some real sense guilty. "In Adam's fall we sinned all."

But how could we have all sinned in Adam?

1. Some adopt the "Realistic Theory" of Augustine and Jonathan Edwards, that billions of human beings were germinally in Adam and wickedly sinned when he sinned. Or we had an existence in Adam, "not as persons but as a simple essence" (Augustine), and are generally involved in the responsibility of the individual.

2. Origen held the notion that we all had a pre-existence, and sinned in our previous state—a notion held also by Dr. Edward Beecher and Julius Muller.

3. Others held the Representative and Federal Headship Theory in various forms. Adam stood as our legal representative, and the sin he committed thousands of years before we were born is held to be justly imputed to us, and we are justly punished for it.

4. Others have been so illogical as to hold to both the realistic and the representative theories, which are mutually exclusive.

Other variations of these theories might be named. They all appeal to this passage of Scripture for proof, and deny to their rivals any standing in Rom. 5:12-21. This fact makes it immensely probably that neither of them has any support here.

They are theological speculations and fictions that are horrible reflections on the justice and goodness of God. They are without any sure foundation in Scripture or sound reason, and are more unsubstantial than moonshine.

There is another view which accounts for all the facts without affronting man's moral sense or casting any reflections upon the goodness and justice of God. It is called THE THEORY OF THE GENETIC TRANSMISSION OF DE-PRAVITY. It is the familiar "law of heredity" that "like produces like." Adam propagated his depravity, and it has been propagated through all generations. His sin was not in any sense our fault; the natural consequence of it —sickness and death—was not *a penalty* for a sin for which we never could have been responsible. It is only our *misfortune,* which has befallen us through the working of natural and most holy and beneficent law of God.

"Death passed unto all men, for that all sinned." The word "all" does not mean strictly "all" here, as in many other passages of Scripture. Matt. 3:5: "Then went out unto him Jerusalem, and *all* Judea, and *all* the region round about Jordan, and were baptized of him." Now, absolutely *all* did not go, especially the babies, to be baptized. Theologians have argued that if *"all"* sinned and so died, then the babies who died during past ages must

have sinned; therefore they either sinned in Adam or his sin was imputed to them.

But there is no need of any such forced and unnatural, not to say absurd, argument. St. Paul was simply using language in a popular way, as we all do; and little children died, not because they had sinned in some fanciful imaginary way before they were born, but because they were born with the sin-principle in them, and therefore also with the death-principle in them.

But to match this awful misfortune God gave us the grace of an atoning Savior, and we shall see in this discussion that if we became depraved and sinful through Adam we can have a "much more" salvation through Christ. We can become JUSTIFIED AND SANCTIFIED.

"For until the law sin was in the world: but sin is not imputed when there is no law. Nevertheless the death [principle] reigned from Adam until Moses, even over them that had not sinned after the likeness of Adam's transgression, who is a figure of him that was to come" (Rom. 5:13, 14).

In verse 12 the apostle stated one side of a comparison, but does not state the other side till the eighteenth verse. The intervening five verses are logically a parenthesis. The apostle tells the Jews that antithesis is not narrowed to the period of the Mosaic law alone, but covers the whole of human history and the whole race.

In the period between Adam and Moses men did not have the written law of the Israelites, nor the single specific command that Adam had. Had there been no law of any kind there would have been no actual sin. ("Sin" is without the article in verse 13.) Nevertheless, the sin-principle existed and the death-principle reigned. There was the light of nature, described in the first and second chapters, and also what light came to them, hand-ed down by tradition. The light they did not follow. The sin-principle generally reigned, and death and ruin fol-lowed in its train.

The expression "death reigned" is very striking. It is a personification of death as a monarch, having domin-ion over all that period and over all those generations. Under his dark and withering reign men went down to death, conquered by the "king of terrors." "Were it not for the atoning Savior and His mighty Gospel of full salvation, this dread power would bring unmitigated woes upon the earth, and his silent tread and resistless sceptre would cause only desolation and woe for ever."

Adam is a "figure of Him that was to come." That is, there may be instituted a comparison between the results of Adam's sin and Christ's atonement. It is mainly by way of contrast that the comparison is instituted as the following verses show:

Verse 15: *"For if by the trespass of the one the many died,* MUCH MORE *did the grace of God, and the gift by the grace of the one Man, Jesus Christ, abound unto the many."*

This is a contrast in quality.

(1) It was *trespass* in one: it was *holiness* in the other.

(2) A *curse* came through the one: grace came through the other; and it abounded *"much more,"* so that greater benefits have resulted from the work of Christ than evils from the fall of Adam.

Verse 16: *"And not as through one that sinned, so is the gift: for the judgment came of one unto condemna-tion, but the free gift came of many trespasses unto justi-fication."*

The contrast here is in numbers.

(1) The sin was of *one man*: the grace comes to *all* men.

(2) The judgment was for *one* sin: the grace is offered to cover the *multitude of sins* of the multitude of men.

Verse 17: *"For if, by the trespass of the one, death reigned through the one;* MUCH MORE *shall they that receive the abundance of grace and of the gift of righteousness reign in life through the One, even Jesus Christ."*

The contrast here is in result.

(1) The trespass of Adam brought *death*: but the grace of Christ brings *life*.

(2) The ravage of death is limited: but they who receive the abundance of grace in Christ shall reign in life "much more"—even for ever.

And it is a *gift*, to be received voluntarily and freely. To infants and irresponsible beings the grace and gift are unconditional. To free agents it is offered gratuitously. Nothing but man's voluntary rejection of the offer can deprive him of eternal life through Christ.

Verse 18: *"So then as through one trespass the judgment came unto all men to condemnation; even so through one act of righteousness the free gift came unto all men to justification of life."*

(1) Adam committed *one* trespass: Christ forgives *many* trespasses.

(2) Adam brought *judgment*: Christ brought *justification*.

(3) Adam's curse fell upon "ALL MEN": Christ's free gift came to "ALL MEN."

It is difficult to believe that God would have allowed our first parent to propagate a depraved race, if He had not provided for its cure by the atonement of Christ. So grace was provided on the day of the fall, before a child was born; and the curse and the cure have come together down the ages.

As the work of Christ does not wholly save the race unless it is embraced by personal faith, so the deed of Adam, while it brings sorrow and loss, does not bring criminality and final ruin unless there is some wicked conduct of our own. It is not any imaginary imputed sin that destroys us, but our own "many trespasses" (verse 16). We must act to be damned by Adam: we must act to be saved by Christ.

Verse 19: *"For as through the one man's disobedience the many were made sinners even so through the obedience of the One shall the many be made righteous."*

Here we will let Alford speak: "By the disobedience of one man the many were made sinners (not 'were accounted as,' not *'became so by imputation,'* nor 'were proved to be'—the kind of sin spoken of in this whole passage is both original and actual—but 'were made sinners'), actual sinners by practice. So by Christ shall the many be made righteous; *not by imputation merely, any more than in the other case,* BUT SHALL BE MADE REALLY AND ACTUALLY RIGHTEOUS, AS COMPLETELY SO AS THE OTHERS WERE MADE REALLY AND ACTUALLY SINNERS. Man *in Christ* and united to Him is *made righteous,* not by a fiction, nor by imputation only of Christ's righteousness, but by a real and living spiritual union with a righteous Head, as a righteous member, righteous by *means of,* as an effect of, the righteousness of that Head, but not merely righteous by transference of the righteousness of that Head."

Reader, to be made "actually righteous" by Christ means to be *sanctified;* means to have *"the sin,"* inherited from Adam, taken away by the mightier Christ.

Verse 20: *"And the law came in besides, that the trespass might abound; but where the sin abounded, the grace did abound more exceedingly: . . ."*

When the law came it deepened the sinfulness of sins, aggravated the carnal nature of men, and stirred them up to trespass still more. But where sins multiplied, grace in Christ abounded much more.

The Gospel offers full pardon for all that is past. All the transgressions for which the soul is condemned to death are forgiven freely. And more, the Holy Spirit is sent by Christ to cleanse the heart from the indwelling sin, and impart His gifts and graces, and prepare for service here and heaven hereafter.

Thus the grace of the Gospel not only redeems from death and restores to life, but brings the soul into such a relationship with God, and such a glorious character and destiny, as we have no authority to believe ever would have been ours, nor even Adam's, if he had never sinned. So the *abounding sin* is over-matched by the *abounding grace.*

Verse 21: *"That as the sin reigned in death, even so might the grace reign through righteousness unto eternal life through Jesus Christ our Lord."*

Here, as Dr. Maclaren observes, we have "The warring Queens. The Sin and the Grace are both personified. They stand face to face, and each recognizes as her enemy the other. The one has established her dominion: 'The Sin hath reigned.' The other is fighting to establish hers: 'That the Grace might reign.' And the struggle is going on in the heart of each of us. The Sin stands there, a hideous hag. The Grace stands here, in all her gestures, dignity and love. This antagonist Queen is nothing but the love of God in exercise to sinful men."

And how can this Divine Queen give us a "much-more" salvation, unless she can conquer and destroy that old hag of SINFUL PROPENSITY? But exactly this is her self-allotted task. She proposes to *sanctify* us, and *"reign through righteousness unto eternal life."* This is the real need of the world. Says Dr. Maclaren, "The thing that the world wants is to have sin dealt with . . . in the way of drying up its source and delivering men from the power of it. Unless you do that you but pour a bottleful of cold water into Vesuvius and try to put the fire out with that. You may educate, you may cultivate, you may refine; you may set political and economical arrangements right in accordance with the newest notions of the century: and what then? Why, the old thing will just begin over again, and the old miseries will appear over again, because the old grandmother of them all is there, '*The* Sin' that has led to them. You may have high education, beautiful refinement of culture and manners; you may give everybody 'a living wage,' and the world will groan still because you have not dealt with the taproot of all the mischief. You cannot kill an internal cancer with a plaster on the little finger; and you will never stanch the world's wounds until you go to the Physician, Jesus Christ, that TAKES AWAY 'THE SIN' of the world. What each of us wants, before we can see the Lord, is that something shall lay hold of us, and utterly change our natures, and *express from our hearts that black drop that lies there tainting everything."*

Precisely that is what Jesus proposes to do, and must do, or His salvation is a failure.

Inevitable Consequences
What Depends upon Choice on Both Sides

First Adam	Second Adam or Christ
1. Depravity at birth for all.	1. Birth in realm of grace for all.
2. Physical death for all.	2. Resurrection for all.
3. Pains and sorrows for all.	3. Helping grace for all.
4. Possibility of eternal death for all.	4. Possibility of eternal life for all.
5. Disaster from one sin to all.	5. Provisional salvation from all sins to all.
6. Mental and spiritual darkness upon all.	6. The light that lighteth every man that cometh into the world.
7. The condemnation.	7. The free gift.
8. The sin abounded, depravity in all.	8. The grace did much more abound in sanctification for all, and heaven.
1. No guilt from sin of Adam, until endorsed by our own choice of sin.	1. No salvation from Christ's righteousness until endorsed by our choice of salvation.
2. No responsibility for possession of depravity until remedy is rejected.	2. No escape from the depravity through Adam's sin till the remedy is accepted.
3. In spite of all misfortunes from Adam, no hell except by our own choice of sin.	3. Notwithstanding all Jesus has done for salvation, no heaven but by our own free choice.
4. The sin hath reigned (by consent).	4. The grace may reign (by consent).

CHAPTER III

"What shall we say then? Shall we continue in THE SIN, *that* THE GRACE *may abound? God forbid: we who died in the sin, how shall we live any longer therein?"* (Rom. 6:12).

Paul is making his most masterly argument for complete salvation by faith. He has just said in Rom. 5:20, "Where *the sin abounded, the grace* did abound more exceedingly: that, as *the sin* reigned in death, even so might *the grace* reign through righteousness unto eternal life through Jesus Christ our Lord." But the carnal heart perverts every truth of God, and the apostle knew that this would be perverted. He foresaw that men would argue, and doubtless he had heard them argue, for continuance in a life of sin as follows: "Very well! If where sin abounds grace much more abounds, then let us continue in sin, and sin abundantly, for so God can have a chance to make more glorious displays of His grace."

People are making the same kind of argument now. They are smiling upon the sin quite generally in our churches, treating it as a light matter, and thus presume on God's grace. They will tell you, in the face of God's commands to the contrary, that holiness is not at all essential. We can keep on sinning, for there is plenty of grace. Some are even making continuous sinning a necessity. A famous catechism tells us, "No man is able either of himself or by any grace received in this life, to keep the commandments of God, but doth daily break them in thought, word and deed."

27

Thus all confidence in the possibility of an obedient walk with God is paralyzed under the baneful influence of this notion. Professors of religion settle down into a complacent acquiescence in a life of sin, and make the duty of personal holiness a subject of joke and derision.

Now the whole sixth chapter of Romans is St. Paul's spirited protest against, and sharp rebuke of, such a Satanic conclusion.

In this discussion let us consider

I. What is "the sin"?

The Greek noun for sin with the definite article before it occurs fourteen times in this chapter, and gives the key to the argument. Let it be remembered that we showed in chapter 2, from a large number of commentators, that "the sin" in this passage means *"sin as a principle," "hereditary corruption," "natural depravity," "sinfulness," "a sinful disposition."* Lange says: *"The sin* denotes sin as a power or principle which reveals itself in hereditary corruption."

In this chapter, this *sin principle* is remarkably personified. In the sixth verse it is called "the old man" and "the body of sin." Lange says: "The old man is the whole sinfulness of man that proceeds from Adam." Tholuck says: "It is the tendency of alienation from God." Barnes says: "The old man is a personification of the corrupt propensities of our nature." Lightfoot says: "The old man is the personification of our whole sinful condition before regeneration." We add, "And after regeneration too," because regeneration does not remove it.

In verses 16-20 "the sin is personified as a slave-master driving on his slaves to the commission of all manner of sins." This same idea is continuous throughout this entire section of the epistle. It is manifest then that, while in the earlier part of the epistle the apostle was discussing God's method of *justification* or the *pardon of sins,* here he has advanced to the discussion of the Gospel cure of *the sin principle,* or *sanctification.* This inference is unmistakable, from the words and figures of speech used; and twice in the chapter, verses 19 and 22, he actually names sanctification. The great apostle here lifts up the true Gospel standard of Christian living. He does not treat it as an impracticable ideal of the imagination, impossible to be realized, but as the true ideal within reach of every child of God. He expresses astonishment that any Christian should accept a lower standard. He thus brought the believers of his own time, and *he brings us,* face to face with the abrupt question, "Shall we continue in the sin, in depravity, in the propensity or inclination to sin?" "Shall we remain unclean, unholy, unsanctified, unlike God?"

II. What can it mean to be dead to "the sin"?

The apostle asks: "We who died to sin, how shall we any longer live therein?" *When* did we thus die to sin? The verb is the aorist tense, and refers to some definite act of the past, some change from sin and righteousness. Ellicott appropriately suggests that *"potentially* we died to sin in our Lord's passion, and *actually* (in our purpose) when we accepted Christ as individuals." In other words, in the atonement provision was made for all men to be rid of the curse of sin. Christ died *for* sin, that we might die *to* sin. And in conversion a man consents to abandon sin, and to accept all for which Jesus died. By consent and in the purpose of his heart, "he dies once for all to sin, he lives henceforth forever to God" (Lightfoot). "To live," says Godet admirably, "is not merely to regain peace with God through justification; it is to dwell in the light of His holiness, and to act in permanent communion with Him. In the cure of the soul, pardon is only the crisis of convalescence; the *restoration of health is sanctification. Holiness is true life.*"

But we *experimentally* die to sin as an actual fact when sanctifying grace destroys the abnormal proclivity to sin, and we become dead to the enticements of evil. We have this idea of being dead to sin in the second verse, and the seventh and the eleventh. The critical reader will notice that there is a double death. In the sixth verse "the old man" (*i. e.,* the corrupt propensities of our nature) is crucified, and the *"body of sin"* is destroyed: but in the eleventh verse the figure is changed, and it is the Christian who dies "to the sin" as his master. It is probably a reciprocal crucifixion like that mentioned by Paul in Gal. 6:14: "God forbid that I should glory, save in the Cross of our Lord Jesus Christ, through which the world hath been crucified unto me, and I unto the world."

In view of the context, can such a crucifixion and dying mean anything less than that "the sin," "the old man" of depravity, can be so destroyed by sanctifying grace that the Christian can become as dead to any internal impulse to sin as a corpse is dead to the attractions of the world that once charmed him? A man that is dead is uninfluenced and unaffected by the affairs of this life. He is insensible to sounds and tastes and pleasures. The hum of business does not disturb him. The voices of condemnation or praise do not reach him. All the scenes of commerce or gayety or ambition do not move the heart. The dead orator's breast does not heave at the sound of applause or the tributes of his own eulogy. The dead

warrior's pulse is not quickened by the rattle of musketry
or the roar of cannon or the clash of contending hosts.
And a Christian can be so delivered from the propensity
to be charmed by the world that he is as one dead. The
thing that once stirred within him at the approach of
temptation has been "crucified" and "destroyed," and he
is dead to all but holiness and usefulness and God. So,
we are told three times in this chapter that we are made
free from "the sin."

The great Greek exegete, J. Agar Beet, D. D., says:

"The words 'dead to sin' in the eleventh verse clearly
imply that the old life of sin has completely come to an
end, and the fetters of bondage to sin have been broken.
So complete is the deliverance which St. Paul has in view
that he compares it to Christ's escape by death from the
enemies who nailed Him to the Cross, and from the burden of sin He bore there. Although Himself unspotted by
sin, Christ occupied, during His life on earth, a very real
and painful relation to it, and specifically to *'the sin'* of
the world. In order to save us from death, which is the
consequence of 'the sin,' the Son of God placed Himself
under the curse and burden of sin. During His life He
was exposed to all the deadly assaults of sinful men, and
the powers of darkness who, through them, struck Him.
How real and awful was His contact with sin we see by
His agony in the garden and on the Cross.

"All this explains in what sense Christ died to (in relation to) sin. His awful relation to it was absolutely
sundered by His death. While He lived he was exposed to
the assaults of His foes, and He groaned beneath the curse
of the world's sin. But in the moment of His death He
was free. The taunts and jeers and curses of His enemies

hurt Him no more. In the moment of death He was separated from it all for ever.

"Just so, the words, 'dead to sin,' clearly imply that the old life of sin in the Christian may come to an end, and all the fetters of its bondage be broken. The phrase describes complete deliverance from all bondage and defilement of sin. This verse (eleventh) embodies the all-important and distinctive Christian doctrine of 'sanctification in Christ through faith.' "

We heartily accept the conclusion of that noble Christian scholar. Beyond all question, the subject under discussion here is *"the sin-principle"* and *deliverance from it,* or "SANCTIFICATION." Alford says: "The passage teaches that we shall be made righteous, not by imputation but really and actually righteous, as completely so as we were made really and actually sinners."

III.   Now if we may thus be delivered from "the sin," St. Paul asks, "How shall we live any longer therein?"

This question is practically repeated in the fifteenth verse. The apostle expresses astonishment that anyone should desire it or think of it.

Elliott says: "St. Paul sees the matter in the ideal light to force upon the consciences of his hearers the fact that an entire change came over them when they became Christians—that the knowledge and the grace then vouchsafed to them did not leave them where they were—that they are not, and cannot be, their former selves, and that it is a contradiction of their very being to sin any more."

Whedon says: "Christian faith, in its very essence an act, is an abandonment of *the sin* and a most entire and perfect surrender to holiness."

"Holiness," says Godet, "is salvation in its very essence. Justification is to be regarded as the *strait gate* through which we enter on the *narrow way* of sanctification, which leads to glory." "In this section of the epistle (6:1—7:6) the apostle unfolds the new principle of sanctification contained in the very object of justifying faith —Jesus Christ." . . . "In the previous part of the epistle the thought of the apostle was on the contrast between *wrath* and *justification;* but the contrast here is between the *sin* and *holiness*. For the matter in question is no longer to efface sin as *guilt,* but to overcome it as a *power* or *disease*." . . . "The apostle shows the powerlessness of the law to sanctify as well as to justify; and, on the other hand, the entire sufficiency of the Gospel to accomplish both tasks."

We are happy to be able to quote these three commentators in support of our argument that the apostle is here unfolding *sanctification through the Spirit* as the cure of *"the sin,"* the death of our depravity. Many others might be quoted. We want our readers to know that this is no hair-brained theory of ours, but the real teaching of the Word of God.

The apostle launches out into several arguments to show how abhorrent it is to continue unsanctified and live in "the sin." 1. He says in verses 3-5, IT INVOLVES THE BREAKING OF THE BAPTISMAL VOW. The very rite means a profession of a holy purpose to be dead to *"the sin"* principle, and a vow to live to God. Baptism in the New Testament Church takes the place of circumcision in the Old. The rite of circumcision, as explained in Col. 2:9-11, meant "the putting off of the body of the flesh in the circumcision of Christ." Meyer says: "The spiritual circumcision, divinely performed, consisted in a complete parting and doing away with *this body of sin*, in so far as God has removed the sinful body from a man, like a garment drawn off and laid aside." Now the rite of baptism looks to, and signifies in purpose, the same cleansing of our nature. As Christ died to the curses of mocking men, so we in baptism profess to be willing to die to this inward curse of sin: as Christ rose again, so we in baptism consent to rise to a holy life.

Am I forcing this argument? Listen to the Prayer Book of the Church of England: "Baptism representeth unto us our profession which is to follow the example of our Savior Christ, and to be made like unto Him: that as He died and rose again for us, so should we, who are baptized, die for sin, and rise again unto righteousness."

The Southern Methodist Episcopal Church has this prayer in her baptismal ceremony: "O merciful God, grant that the Old Adam in these persons may be so buried that the new man may be raised up in them. Amen. Grant that all carnal affections may die in them, and that all things belonging to the Spirit may live in them. Amen."

Alford says: "The apostle refers to an acknowledged fact in the signification of baptism—that it put upon us a state of conformity with and participation in Christ; and that this involves A DEATH TO SIN *even as He died to sin.*" Now, for such baptized Christians to spurn sanctification and refuse to be rid of their carnality is to renounce their own baptism and to do violence to all its sacred meaning.

2. The apostle teaches in the sixth verse that TO REFUSE SANCTIFICATION, AND PURPOSELY CONTINUE TO LIVE IN "THE SIN," IS TO REJECT THE ATONEMENT IN ITS RESULTS. Provisionally, "our old man was crucified with

him, that *the body of* THE SIN *might* be destroyed." This
was the sacred purpose of Christ's death. Eph. 5:25:
"Christ loved the church, and gave himself up for it;
that he might *sanctify* it, having *cleansed* it . . . that it
should be holy and without blemish." Heb. 13:12: "Jesus
also, that he might sanctify the people with his own blood,
suffered without the gate."

In 1 John 1:7 we are told that "The blood of Jesus
Christ, his Son, cleanseth us from all sin."

Now, when we learn that God has set His heart on our
being free from "the sin," and Jesus shed His life's blood
on the cross that we might be thus sanctified, if we spurn
this blessing and cling to our "old man" of carnality,
what else is it than treading under foot the Son of God,
and counting the blood of the covenant wherewith we
might be sanctified an unholy thing, and doing despite to
the Spirit of grace?

Remember what this old man is. Dr. Barnes voices a
dozen commentators when he says, "It is a personification
of the corrupt propensities of our nature"; or, as Tholuck
says: "Our *tendency* of alienation from God." This is the
vile fountain from which the stream of sin flows. This is
the traitor in the citadel of the soul, which responds to
every outside solicitation to evil and longs to deliver us
into the hands of our enemies. This is the internal cancer
that eats away at the spiritual life, to consume it utterly.
"For from within," said Jesus, "out of the heart of men,
evil thoughts proceed, fornications, thefts, murders, adul-
teries, covetings, wickedness, deceit, lasciviousness, an
evil eye, railing, pride, foolishness: all these proceed from
within and defile the man." This is the *"bent to back-
sliding"* in the hearts of unsanctified believers, of which
God justly complains. This is "the root of bitterness" by

which so many Christian hearts are despoiled of their loveliness. This is what expresses itself in the easily besetting sin, in the fierce uprising of ungovernable temper, and in the smoldering embers of hate. Oh, this is that "carnal mind that is enmity against God," and will not bow to God and tries to keep us from doing it, and is the relentless foe of all deep spirituality in every life.

And this "*old man* was crucified with Christ, that this *body of sin* might be destroyed." That is to say, Jesus in His atoning work made provision for this old thing to be crucified, that this *propensity to sin* "MIGHT BE DE-STROYED." Barnes says: "It refers to the *moral destruction* of the power of sin in the heart by the gospel, and not to any physical change in the nature."

Now, when any Christian understands this truth, and then deliberately rejects this cleansing, sanctifying grace, and refuses to have his carnality destroyed, what better is it than to stand on Calvary and join the rabble crowd of Christ-rejecters who mock the dying agonies of the Son of God?

3. The apostle further shows that TO CONTINUE IN "THE SIN" INVOLVES A DISREGARD OF GOD'S GLORY. The more wretched sinners become like God, the more glory He will get out of us. It will reveal Jesus as a mighty Savior, and will display to an admiring universe the glories of His redemption.

Verse 7: "For he that is dead is freed from sin" (old ver.). New ver.: "Justified from sin." Barnes: "The word here is used in the sense of setting at liberty, or destroying the power or dominion," "as a master ceases to have power over a slave when he is dead." Lange: "It means a release from sin by the death of the sinner himself." Clarke says: "The context shows that it means,

'All his evil propensities are destroyed, and he is WHOLLY SANCTIFIED TO GOD'."

Verses 8-11 confirm what has been said before: *"If we be dead with Christ."* Barnes: *"If we are made dead to sin* by Christ's atoning work, as He was dead in the grave." *"We believe we shall also live with Him."* "It refers not to the future so much as the present. It becomes an article of our belief that we are to live with Christ. As He was raised from death, so we shall be raised from the death of sin. As He lives, so we shall live in holiness." And God expects it of us here and now (1 Peter 1:15). Whedon: "Dead to a world of sin, as Christ was dead to a world of external things, and live with Him—that is, live in conformity with His character."

Verse 10: *"He died unto [in relation to] THE SIN once [for all]: but the life that he liveth he liveth unto God."* The death of Christ was the very highest point of antagonism between holiness and *the sin.* Barnes observes: "The design of His death was to destroy sin. . . . The whole force of the motive, therefore, drawn from the death of Christ is to induce Christians to forsake sin. And Christ now lives 'unto God'—that is, to advance His glory; so should the powers of Christians, being raised from the death of sin, be exerted to promote the glory of God." But very little glory can God get out of Christians who of choice remain carnal. "The sin" holds so large a place in human life that it will not be innocently, ineffectively dormant. It shows itself to be a most aggressive force in a little child, and it grows in effective virulence in the after years. Without complete victory over *the sin* there can be no unreserved devotion to God; for all is resistance to God. So God proposes to "crucify," "destroy" this foul thing within, that we may have no

more trouble with it, and have perfect leisure to devote
ourselves to the glory of God.

Rom. 7:11: *"Even so reckon ye also yourselves to be
dead unto the sin, but alive unto God in Christ Jesus."*
With the end of Jesus' life, His struggle with sin ended.
Even so, says the apostle, let your relation with sin end.
Godet says on this and following verses: "As Christ does
not return back again from His life in glory (to have relation to sin), so the believer, once dead to sin and alive to
God in Christ, cannot return to his old life of sin. . . . The
believer does not get disentangled from sin gradually. He
breaks with it in Christ once for all. He is placed by a de-
cisive act of will (and the work of the Spirit) in the sphere
of perfect holiness. . . . This second gospel paradox, SANC-
TIFICATION BY FAITH, rests on the first, JUSTIFICATION BY
FAITH."

Professor Dougan Clark, D.D., says on this passage:
"We are wholly unable to destroy or do away with the
body of sin by any resolution or will-power of our own.
The sin will not go dead at our bidding, nor can we become dead to it by wishing or striving to be so. Again,
we are brought face to face with our helplessness, but
the apostle solves our problem for us by directing us to re-
sort to the process of *reckoning*. What we reckon with
the sublime reckoning of faith, Christ can make real and
true.

But we must not fail to reckon ourselves *alive* as well
as *dead*. And to be *alive* to God means to be responsive to
every intimation of His will—in short, to be SANCTIFIED
WHOLLY. Oh, beloved, what a blessed reckoning is the
reckoning of faith! How vastly does it transcend all the
reckonings of logic or mathematics! For by it we experience a deadness to sin and a holiness of heart and life."

The sainted Friend, David B. Updegraff, says: "I hated pride, ambition, evil tempers, and vain thoughts, but I had them, and they were a part of me not as acts, but as dispositions lying behind the acts, and promptings thereto, natural to the 'old man.' . . . But, with my all upon the altar, I had no sooner 'reckoned myself dead unto [the] sin, and alive unto God,' than the 'Holy Ghost fell' upon me. Instantly I felt the melting and refining fire of God permeating my whole being."

Agar Beet, D.D., the noted Greek exegete, says: "St. Paul bids us reckon it to be ours. This reckoning implies full assurance. For when a reckoning is complete, the reckoner knows the result. . . . This verse embodies the all-important and distinctively Christian doctrine of SANCTIFICATION IN CHRIST THROUGH FAITH."

Verses 12 and 13: *"Let not sin therefore reign in your mortal body . . . neither present your members unto the sin."* In other words, "Therefore," since you can get rid of *the sin* by the sanctifying grace of Christ, do it, and do not let it reign in you any more, nor yield your members to its use.

"The sin" is again personified as a ruler, or queen. Adam Clarke says: "Let not the sin have any place or being in your soul. . . . Wherever the sin is felt, there the sin has dominion; for sin is sin only as it works in *action* or passion against God. The sin cannot be a quiescent thing: if it does not work, it does not exist."

Barnes says: "Christians should devote every member of the body to God and His service—the tongue, hands, feet, eyes, ears, etc., all for God."

Verse 13: *"But present yourselves unto God, as alive from the dead, and your members as instruments of righteousness unto God."* Here the apostle names one of the

fundamental conditions of sanctification. Very definitely
"PRESENT YOURSELVES"—even minutely YOUR INDIVIDUAL
MEMBERS—to God in entire consecration. In verse 11 he
has just urged Christians to exercise faith for the blessing
of sanctification. But it is impossible for an unconsecrat-
ed person to exercise any such sanctifying faith. Now,
in this verse he shows how to get all difficulty out of the
way. Jesus takes all He can get, and sanctifies all who
will let Him. Jesus is the altar whereon we place ourselves
as a sacrifice, and "what soever toucheth the altar is made
holy." Jesus himself said, "The altar sanctifieth the gift."
It is the personal transaction of a heart already regenerated—"alive from the dead"—with a personal God, for
the sake of holiness and the greater glory of a sanctifying
Savior.

Professor Dougan Clark says: "The essence of consecration is in the sentence, 'Yield yourselves unto God.'
When you yield yourselves you yield everything else. All
the details are included in the one surrender of yourself:
'Yield yourself unto God.' Consecration is not to God's
service, not to His *work,* not to a life of *obedience* and
sacrifice, not to the *Church,* not to the *Christian Endeavor*
not to the *missionary cause,* nor even to the *cause of God*:
it is to GOD HIMSELF. Consecration is the willingness, and
the resolution, and the purpose to be, to do, and to suffer
all God's will." The verb is in the aorist tense, and denotes a definite transaction, made once for all, never to
be repeated, unless we have failed to keep it.

Meyer says: "The imperative aorist denotes the *in-
stantaneousness* with which the consecration of the body
should be carried out."

Philippi: "This tense expresses the idea of a consecration *once for all.*"

Godet says: "It indicates an *immediate transition* into the new state. This change should affect not the body only, but the whole person, Yield yourselves.' All is included in that of the person." . . . According to Lange and Schaff the sanctification of the mortal body here below is mentioned as serving to prepare for its glorification above."

Professor Isaiah Reid gives this form of consecration for holiness: "O Lord, in view of this thing Thou hast besought me to do, I hereby do now really consecrate myself unreservedly to Thee, for all time and eternity. My time, my talents, my hands, feet, lips, will, my all. My property, my reputation, my entire being, a living sacrifice to be and to do all Thy righteousness will pertaining to me. Especially at this time do I, Thy regenerate child, put my case into Thy hands for the cleansing of my nature from indwelling sin. I seek the sanctification of my soul."

He adds this pledge of faith: "Now, as I have given myself away, I will, from this time forth, regard myself as Thine. I believe Thou dost accept the offering I bring. I put all on the altar. I believe the altar sanctifieth the gift. I believe the blood is applied now, as I comply with the terms of Thy salvation. I believe that Thou DOST NOW CLEANSE ME FROM ALL MY SIN."

Any regenerated person who thus consecrates for this blessing has a right to believe, on the promises of God, that He does then and there keep His word and cleanse the heart. Yea, it would be dishonoring God NOT TO BELIEVE.

Verses 14, 15: *"For sin shall not have dominion over you: for ye are not under law but under grace. What then? Shall we sin, because we are not under law but under grace? God forbid."*

The word "sin" has no such article in verse 14, as if it referred to an act, although, as Barnes and other commentators admit, it is personified here as previously, and still refers to "the propensity or inclination to sin." Perhaps the reason of the change is revealed in the tense of the verb in the fifteenth verse. According to Lange, Meyer, Tischendorf, Godet, and others, the true reading is *"hamartesomen"*—aorist subjunctive of *deliberation,* not a future, and is best rendered *"may* we sin."

Godet makes this fine comment: "The principle of holiness inherent in salvation has been demonstrated. . . . The question which now arises is whether this new dominion (of sanctifying grace) will be strong enough to banish sin *in every particular case.* Hence the form of the aorist subjunctive: *should we commit an* (one) *act of sin?* Could we act thus voluntarily in a single instance?" "GOD FORBID." "LET IT NOT BE SO." Hallelujah! How much better and more scriptural that sounds than the rattle of an old creed which tells us that we must "sin daily in thought, word, and deed" as long as we live! Such an assertion is unbiblical, contradictory to God, and insulting to the sanctifying Holy Ghost. If the Bible teaches anything, it teaches that sin is not a necessity. No act of sin can be necessary in a moral universe ruled over by a holy God.

IV. Paul teaches in the sixteenth and following verses that to continue in "the sin" and yield to it and refuse deliverance is to be "the sin's" slave.

Verse 16: *"Know ye not that to whom ye yield yourselves as servants, unto obedience, his servants ye are whom ye obey; whether of sin unto death, or of obedience unto righteousness?"*

Here, as in verse 14, the word "sin" is without the article, the only times in the entire chapter. The personification of sin is still kept up. But the article may be omitted for a purpose. Godet suggests: "Paul seemed to hear the objection that an act of God's grace is enough to annul it, so that not a trace of it shall remain. So superficial Pelagianism understands moral liberty. After the doing of each act it can return to the state in which it was before, exactly as if nothing had passed. But a more serious study of human life proves, on the contrary, that every act of will, whether in the direction of good or evil, creates or strengthens a tendency which drags men with increasing force till it becomes altogether irresistible." The first sin of Adam created his depravity. The first sin of a sanctified Christian would again reproduce a *tendency to sin*. So a fully saved person should shrink from sinning even once again.

If men yield themselves to commit a sin they create a propensity and become the servants of it. They then give themselves to the indulgence of it, even with death and ruin and condemnation before them. They follow their evil propensities even if they lead them to hell. So it is never safe to commit one sin. That way is death.

"So," says Barnes, "the same law exists in regard to holiness or obedience. The man who becomes the servant of holiness will feel himself bound by the law of servitude to obey, unto eternal life." "The word 'righteousness' in this verse means PERSONAL HOLINESS."

Verse 17: *"But thanks be to God that whereas ye were servants of the sin, ye became obedient from the heart to that form of teaching whereunto ye were deliv-*

ered." These men had been in the bondage to the sin—completely its slaves. But they had been set free by heart-obedience to the gospel. Like every other body of believers, they were in various stages of grace. Some probably were sanctified, and all were urged to be. For the next verse reads:

Verse 18: *"Being then made free from the sin, ye became the servants of righteousness."* "The aorist participle here," says Lange, "denotes a definite act of deliverance." That is exactly what we are contending for, that in sanctification we get definite deliverance from the sin-principle, and this great truth is taught in a striking and solemn way in this and the following verses of this chapter. For

V. St. Paul shows that self-interest should prompt us to dissolve all relationship with this internal sinfulness.

"Ye became servants." "You became voluntarily under the dominion of righteousness: you yielded yourselves to it: and ye are therefore bound to be holy" (Barnes). Here is "the sin" personified as a slave-master, and the manumission from slavery. The slave, once set free from his servitude, is as free as if he had never been a slave. So is the Christian who is once set free from the sin.

Verse 19: *"As ye have yielded your members as servants to uncleanness and to iniquity unto iniquity, even so now present your members servants of righteousness unto sanctification."* Formerly they had yielded all the faculties of their being to the service of the sin-principle to commit iniquity; even so now they should present all their members to their new master—righteousness, to practice sanctification. Godet suggests: "There is a slightly ironical touch here. It concerns Christians to be as zealous servants to their new master as they formerly were in the service of their old master. 'Ye were eager to yield your members to sin, to commit evil, be ye now as eager to yield them to righteousness, to realize holiness. Do not inflict on this second master the shame of serving him less faithfully than the first.' "

Dr. Barnes says: "Let the surrender of your members to holiness be as sincere and as unqualified as the surrender was to sin. This is all that is required of Christians. If all would employ the same energies in advancing the kingdom of God that they have in promoting the kingdom of Satan, the Church would rise with dignity and grandeur, and every continent and island would soon feel the movement. No requirement is more reasonable than this; and it should be a source of lamentation and mourning with Christians that it is not so; that they have employed so mighty energies in the cause of Satan, and do so little in the service of God." This is sadly true, and we see no cure for it but this great blessing of sanctification which will take out of Christians their carnality and selfishness, and get them all on fire with a passion for souls.

This is the very remedy that St. Paul suggests. He makes an argument for energy in the divine life by comparing the rewards obtained in the two kinds of servitude. "Yield your members servants of righteousness unto SANCTIFICATION."

Verse 20: *"For when ye were servants of the sin ye were free in regard to righteousness."*

Verse 21: *"What fruit then had ye at that time in the things whereof ye are now ashamed? for the end of those things is death."*

What an awful statement! When a man has this carnality in him and he consents to serve it, it empties him of
all goodness and makes him wholly displeasing to God.
"Free from righteousness!" Carnality incarnate! A
moral leper, ready for death! But such will Christians
become who deliberately reject this priceless blessing of
sanctification and choose to be slaves of the sin.

Verse 22: *"But now being made free from the sin*
(aorist tense, once for all) *and become servants to God*
(aorist tense, once for all) *ye have* (*continually,* present
progressive tense)*your fruit unto sanctification, and the
end eternal life."* What a galaxy of glorious truths are
brought together here! (1) We can be definitely set free
from this cruel old tyrant, *the sin-principle,* delivered
from him so instantaneously and completely that he will
trouble us no more. (2) *"Being made free"* by Christ our
mighty Deliverer, the "LION OF THE TRIBE OF JUDAH."
"THE LAMB OF GOD that taketh away 'THE SIN' of the
world." Performing His High-Priestly office, He baptizeth us with the Holy Spirit, *"cleansing our hearts by
faith"* (Acts 15:8, 9). (3) We have our "fruit unto sanctification." The result is sanctification. That is what
sanctification is—a state of freedom from the principle
of sin, "the carnal mind," the alienation from God, the
proneness to sin! Oh, wonderful deliverance! And (4)
we can have it "NOW." It is not something that we get
by development and growth. The cleansing of our heart
is the work of the Holy Spirit performed "suddenly" as
at Pentecost. We do not get it by the discipline of life
and the passage of years. The writer once heard an old
lady, eighty years old, testify as follows: "I was converted when I was ten years old. I tried to grow into sanctification for sixty-nine years, and utterly failed. Then

I got tired of trying to get it by growth, and last year I went to that altar and received it by faith in half an hour, and I have the blessing yet." That was the scriptural way. The Holy Word always tells us that we receive the Spirit by *faith*, and are *sanctified by faith*. Sanctification is purity of heart, freedom from the indwelling sin, obtained instantaneously. Then we grow to MATURITY, and will grow for ever.

Much less do we get sanctified by death. One writer says: "The body of sin in believers is indeed an enfeebled, conquered, and deposed tyrant, and the stroke of death finishes its destruction." Indeed! Then the Omnipotent Christ and the Infinite Spirit can only enfeeble indwelling sin; but physical death can finish him and sanctify us wholly. Thus not Jesus but death becomes our Savior. "The sin" produced death, and death, the effect of sin, turns about and destroys its cause! This is only heathen philosophy, rank with absurdity! No! "May the God of peace himself sanctify you wholly" (1 Thess. 5:23). It is God that does it, and not death, and He does it instantaneously. Sanctification is as instantaneous as justification. Each is performed by an act of God in response to our faith.

And (5) this sanctification ends in heaven. The final result, the ultimate consequence, is "eternal life." By this tremendous consideration the great apostle would inspire all believers to seek deliverance from *the sin* and be sanctified wholly, and be preserved blameless, ready for their summons to their eternal home.

Verse 23: *"For the wages of the sin is death; but the free gift of God is eternal life in Christ Jesus our Lord."* One can cling to *the sin* and serve it if he likes; but let him not be deceived or disappointed about the wages.

The wages is death; not something arbitrary and unde-
served, but *earned*. Barnes "Not a pain will be inflicted
on the sinner which he does not deserve. Not a sinner
will die who ought not to die. Sinners in hell will be
treated just as they deserve to be treated; and there is
not to man a more fearful and terrible consideration than
this. No man can conceive a more dreadful doom than
for himself to be treated for ever just as he deserves to
be. Death, eternal banishment from God, is the wages
of *the sin* because it was promised, and will be paid in full.

"But eternal life is the free gift of God in Christ Jesus
our Lord." A gift of God, because no man could ever earn
it; but in Christ Jesus He offers His sanctifying grace
freely to every believer who will have it. The cleansed
and holy heart which it gives us is the great preparation
to meet God, and dwell with Him for ever.

Thus the great apostle appeals to us, even by self-in-
terest and the motives drawn from the eternal world and
the contrasted issues of soul-destiny, to accept deliverance
from *the sin* and receive a holy heart, and be forever fitted for companionship with God.

Reader, St. Paul's question, "Shall we live any longer
in sin?" presses for an answer. Shall we accept sanctification and walk with God and gain heaven? Or shall
we refuse our interest in the atonement of Christ, cling
to our carnality, and reap its wages of eternal death?
John Fletcher said: "So much of indwelling sin as we
carry about with us, so much of indwelling hell, so much
of the sting which pierces the damned, so much of the
spiritual fire which will burn up the wicked. To plead,
therefore, for the continuance of indwelling sin is no better than to plead for keeping within your hearts one of
the sharpest stings of death, and one of the hottest coals

of hell-fire. On the other hand, to obtain Christian per-
fection is to have the last feature of Belial's image erased
from your loving souls, the last bit of the sting of death
extracted from your composed breasts, and the last spark
of hell-fire extinguished in your peaceful bosoms."

St. Paul said: "The sting of death is *the sin.*" It is
carnality in the heart that makes it hard for people to die.
John Wesley said: "Our people die well." Certainly.
Sanctified people always die well, for the sting of death
is gone.

Well, here is the apostle's question, "Shall we live any
longer in *the sin?*" What will you do about it? God now
waits for your decision.

CHAPTER IV

THE WRETCHED MAN AND THE WARRING LAW

The seventh chapter of Romans has been a favorite battleground of theologians and a subject of widely different interpretations. Its general purpose is plain. In the early part of the Epistle the great apostle has shown the insufficiency of law to justify; but we can be justified by faith in Christ. And *"much more,"* the ruin of the race of Adam can be repaired by Christ. We can be sanctified (chapter 5). In the sixth chapter he shows that it is both our privilege and our duty to be sanctified. Provision has been made for it by the atonement of Christ, and "the sin" in us so detrimental and dangerous, and so fatal in its end, that we ought by all means to get rid of it. Sanctification or death!

In this seventh chapter he shows that we never can get sanctified by *law*. Law was incapable of justifying a race of sinners: it equally fails everywhere in producing peace and sanctification in any life. And the fault is not in the law. It is holy and just and spiritual: it sharply condemns in us everything unlike God. Therefore it arouses carnality in us to activity, but cannot free us from the power and presence of "the sin." (So interpret Barnes, Whedon, Clarke, and Godet on 7:7-25.)

Chapter 7:16. The apostle shows that the Christian, with the experience depicted in the sixth chapter, is emancipated from servility to law. By his new life in the Redeemer he walks in the paths of holiness under no compulsion of law, but spontaneously and of his own free

50

will. As the deceased husband was physically dead to the wife, so the widow was legally dead to the husband: that is, she was emancipated from all subjection to him or relation to him. Similarly, by the apostle's varied and flexible use of the word *dead* he teaches that we, in our effort to be sanctified and live a holy life, are emancipated from the law and are married to Christ, a new Husband, by relation with whom we are to bear the fruit of holiness (verse 4). We never could bear such fruit through marriage with law: for (verse 5) it only excited all the propensities to sin which worked in all our members to secure gratification. This rebellious indulgence of propensities "brought forth fruit unto death." This was our experience when "in the flesh" (*sarx*), the unregenerate state. But now (verse 6) we are dead to the law— delivered from it as a means of holiness, and live with the new Husband, Christ, in a "newness of spirit."

Then comes the remarkable, much-debated passage, in which Paul defends the law but shows its powerlessness by relating his experience (verses 7-25).

Some of the conflicting views have been that

(1) The rest of this chapter is the picture of an unregenerate man. So the early fathers taught, and Augustine prior to his controversy with the Pelagians.

(2) It is a picture of a regenerate man's experience —Augustine's later view, Jerome, Luther, and Calvin, etc. This view is untenable, for

(a) It opposes all the Bible descriptions of a Christian. In no part of God's Word is a child of God described as a poor carnal slave, "sold under sin."

(b) It would make the gospel as great a failure as the law to redeem a soul.

(3) Some divide the passage, and hold that verses
7-13 treat of the unregenerate experience, and verses
14-25 describe the regenerate experience. So Barnes and
Philippi. But this is open to the same objections as the
second view.

(4) Hodge and some others hold that "there is not
an expression from the beginning to the end of section
verses 14-25 which the holiest man may not and must not
adopt." In other words, "it is St. Paul at his best." This
view is monstrous and utterly untenable, for,

(a) The seventh chapter is in sharp contrast with the
sixth and eighth.

(b) It contradicts all St. Paul has said about his
Christian experience in his epistles. In 1 Cor. 2:16 he
had "the mind of Christ." In 1 Cor. 2:12 he gloried that
"in holiness and sincerity of God he behaved himself."
In 1 Thess. 2:10 he called others and "God also to witness how holily and righteously and unblamably" he had
behaved, and so on. There is no comfort in this passage
for those who want to reject holiness.

(5) Others hold that here Paul introduces himself as
the personification of a legal Jew, who seeks sincerely to
fulfill the law without ever being successful in satisfying
his conscience.

(6) A few restrict the application of the passage to
the apostle's own person. Of these Godet seems to be the
clearest and soundest of all: "The truth is, the whole is
related about *himself,* but with the conviction that his experience will infallibly be that of every Israelite and of
every man who will seriously use the moral law or Mosaic
law as a means of sanctification." . . . "Paul speaks about
the unregenerate man, without concerning himself with
the question how far the unregenerate heart (depravity)

still remains in the regenerate believer. He describes man as he is by nature, man as he knew him. . . . Here is the permanent essence of human nature since the Fall, outside the action of faith. Thus is explained the use of the *present* tense, without our saying that Paul describes his present state." . . . "He recalls with wonderful vividness his impressions of former days" . . . "when as a natural man, and consequently also a legal Jew, he was struggling with the sin in his own strength, without other aid than the law, and consequently overcome by the evil instinct, the *flesh*. What he describes then is the law grappling with the evil nature, where these two adversaries encounter one another without the grace of the gospel." . . . "He regards himself as the normal example of what must happen to every man who, in ignorance of Christ, or apart from Him, will take the law in earnest."

Let us now consider the two sections separately.

Verses 7-13. *What? "Is the law sin?"* No, indeed. The trouble was not in the law, but in me. "Howbeit, I had not known THE SIN" which was in me, except the law had forbidden indulgence, and aroused it. So Ovid said: "The strongest propensity is excited toward that which is prohibited." And again he said: "Vice is provoked by every strong restraint."

Verse 8. *"THE SIN, taking occasion, wrought in me through the commandment all manner of coveting."*

Verse 9. *"And I was alive apart from the law once; but when the commandment came THE SIN revived and I died."* Meyer says: "Paul means his life of childlike innocence." Likewise Godet comments beautifully: "It refers here to the state of a young and pious Israelitish child, trained in the knowledge and love of Jehovah, tasting by faith in the promises of His Word the blessings of

the covenant, awakening and going to sleep in the arms of
the God of his fathers. But from the age of twelve young
Israelites were subjected to legal institutes and became
sons of the law. This brought the crisis to the life of the
young Saul. When he found himself called to apply the
law to his conduct he was not slow to discover sin within
him, for in the depths of his heart he found lust; and not
only did the law unveil this evil principle to him, but it
intensified its power. The torrent bubbled and boiled on
meeting with the obstacle that came in its way." Saul re-
belled and "died" morally. Who killed him? Not the
law; but the law waked up THE SIN, personified here as a
murderer, and it slew him. He sinned by yielding to the
evil propensity, and the internal divorce between God
and him was consummated (verses 10 and 11). *"The holy
commandment, then, instead of leading me to peace and
life, resulted in death: for* THE SIN, *finding occasion, be-
guiled me and slew me."* His corrupt and rebellious propensities, excited by the law, rushed him on into aggravated transgression.

Verse 12. *"So the law is holy, and the commandment
is holy and righteous and good."* But *the indwelling sin* is
the murderer, without which God's law would be benign
and glorious.

Verse 13. *"But* THE SIN *that it might be shown . . .
and became exceeding sinful."* God causes death to follow
sin, in order to unfold the accursedness of THE SIN. Some
make light of it, but "the intrinsic, immutable eternal
execrableness of THE SIN principle is a lesson in theology
which God is continually pressing upon the attention of
men."

Calvin well says, "It was proper that the enormity of
THE SIN should be revealed by the law; because unless it

should break forth by some dreadful and enormous excess, it would not be known to be sin. This excess exhibits itself the more violently, while it turns life into death."

Likewise Barnes says: "The sentiment of the whole is, that the tendency of the law is to excite THE DORMANT SIN of the bosom into active existence, and to reveal its true nature." It is desirable that sin should be thus seen, because

(1) Man should be acquainted with his true character. He should not deceive himself.

(2) Because it is one part of God's plan to develop the secret feelings of the heart, and to show all creatures what they are.

(3 Because only by knowing this will the sinner be induced to take a remedy and strive to be saved. God often thus *suffers* men to plunge into sin, to act out their nature, that they may see themselves and be alarmed at their own character.

Now, this passage teaches that the law of God effectually accomplishes this, but it can go no farther. It is not adapted to sanctify the soul. It would logically follow that the law should be faithfully preached. It is the grand instrument in the hands of a faithful minister to alarm and awaken sinners, and make them cry out for God.

It further follows that all efforts to sanctify yourself —that is, to get rid of indwelling sin by labored efforts to keep the law of God—are utterly vain. Sanctification was never reached in that way. It is an instantaneous work of God, obtained by faith.

Chapter 7:14-25. Dr. Hodge argues that the change of the tenses from past to present in this section indicates that it was Paul's experience at the time of writing, and a picture of any Christian's experience. He thinks that the sentiments expressed in verses 17, 18, 22, and 25 are too exalted for any unrenewed man.

Barnes reaches the same conclusion with regard to the tenses, and that it agrees with the design of Paul's argument, which is to show that the law cannot sanctify.

Dr. Matthew Riddle doubts if the change of tenses can signify so much. He argues that "not until verse 25 is there a distinct Christian utterance, while chapter 8 sounds like a new song of triumph." Dr. Riddle and Lange think "the apostle is not describing a quiescent state, but the process in which man is driven from the law to Christ and an unregenerate person becomes regenerate."

So Olshausen: "The state under the law cannot co-exist with regeneration, and without question, therefore, as chapter 7:24 is to express the awakened need of redemption and verse 25 the experience of redemption itself, verses 14-24 are to be referred to a position *before* regeneration, and to be understood as a description of the conflict within an *awakened* person."

Dr. Clarke thinks that "the theory that this is the experience of all Christians has most pitifully and most shamefully, not only lowered the standard of Christianity, but destroyed its influence and disgraced its character. It would demonstrate the insufficiency of the *gospel* as well as the law."

So thinks Dr. Daniel Steele and Whedon.

John Fletcher says: "St. Paul no more professes himself actually a carnal man in Rom. 7:14 than he professes himself a liar in Rom. 3:7, or James professed to be a curser in James 3:9. It is the figure hypotyposis, so-called in rhetoric, by which writers use the present tense to relate things past or to come, to make narration more lively. It is St. Paul's past in the present tense."

We may admit that something like this struggle with indwelling sin, which St. Paul describes, may and does take place in the breasts of Christians who are not sanctified. But Lange "guards against the thought that this is a distinctively Christian experience. It is the most hopeful state of the unregenerate man; the least desirable state of the regenerate man." It could not be the apostle's best, nor the best possible for any Christian. Whoever advocates such a view, takes refuge behind it to avoid the will of God which is TO BE SANCTIFIED (1 Thess. 4:3).

Godet very truly argues that St. Paul is not here depicting his Christian experience:

(a) For his conversion made a tremendous and radical change in his life which is not even hinted at in the entire passage, and which should have been described between verses 13 and 14;

(b) Because the Holy Spirit, who plays so great a part in a Christian's experience, is not named in the whole section, nor even Jesus himself, whom the apostle so constantly glorified. The contrast between this and the eighth chapter is most striking in this respect.

Godet quotes approvingly M. Bonnet: "The apostle is speaking here neither of the *natural man* in his state of voluntary ignorance and sin, nor of *the child of God,* born anew, set free by grace, and animated by the Spirit of Christ; but of the man whose conscience awakened by the law, has entered sincerely, with fear and trembling, but still *in his own strength,* into the desperate struggle against evil." Godet merely adds: "In *our* actual circumstances the law which thus awakens the conscience and summons it to the struggle against sin, is the law in the form of the gospel, and of the example of Jesus Christ, taken apart from justification in Him and sanctification by Him."

After wading through the wilderness of conflicting opinions in many commentaries, we accept the interpretation of Godet: "The apostle explains what the intervention of the law produced in his own life (verses 7-13), and the state in which, despite his sincere and persevering efforts, it left him (verses 14-23) to issue in that desperate cry of distress in which this state of continual defeats finally expresses itself: WHO SHALL DELIVER ME? Of this liberator he does not know the name at the time when he utters the cry (a fact which proves that he is not yet in the faith); but he anticipates, he hopes for, he appeals to Him without knowing Him. And heaven gives him the answer. Chapter 8 contains this answer: 'The Spirit of Christ hath set me free' (verse 2). He it is that works in me all that the law demanded, without giving me the power to do it (verse 4).

"The passage falls into three cycles, each of which closes with a sort of refrain. It is like a dirge; the most sorrowful elegy that ever proceeded from a human heart. The first cycle embraces verses 14-17. The second, which begins and ends in almost the same way as the first, is contained in verses 18-20. The third differs from the first two in form, but is identical with them in substance; it is contained in verses 21-23, and its conclusion in verses 24, 25 is at the same time that of the whole passage. . . . The repetition of the same thoughts and expressions is, as it were, the echo of the desperate repetition of the same experiences in that legal state wherein man can only shake his chains without succeeding in breaking them. Powerless he writhes to and fro in the prison in which sin and the law have confined him, and in the end can only utter that cry of distress whereby, having exhausted his force for the struggle, he appeals, without knowing Him, to the Deliverer."

First Cycle—

"For we know that the law is spiritual: but I am carnal, sold under THE SIN. *For that which I do, I know not: For what I would, that do I practise; but what I hate, that I do. But if what I would not, that I do, I consent unto the law that it is good. So now it is no more I that do it, but* THE SIN *which dwelleth in me."*

I acknowledge the goodness of the law, but I am a captive. This is not regeneration. The lowest regenerated state has *the sin* rebellious within, but the higher life has carnality underfoot. *The indwelling sin* may gain many masteries, but it never holds permanent dominion over the regenerate man, for then he would cease to be regenerate. But this man is even worse still; he is "sold under THE SIN," not only the subject, but the slave of carnality. And it is not the *base I*, the lower self, but the *higher I* that utters this awful plaint." Says Whedon, "Reducing the hyperbole as much as we reasonably can, it is absolutely inadmissible to predicate this in any case of a regenerate man."

"I am carnal." The best reading here is *sarkinos,* meaning, not carnal in action but carnal "in NATURE." Paul felt a mighty inclination to seek his own gratification in everything. This slave works out the will of his master, follows the blind instincts of corrupted nature which drags him along into evil, and when he sees the result, he abhors it.

Here begins the battle of the I's. It is the corrupt I of carnality and indwelling sin asserting its law in the members, and overwhelming the I of conscience, awakened by the Spirit. What *I* wickedly do, *I* consciously ALLOW NOT. He has in him a tyrant who forces him to act in opposition to his better wishes. What humiliation! What misery!

Second Cycle (verses 18-20)—

"For I know that in me (that is, in my flesh) dwelleth no good thing: for to will is present with me, but to do that which is good is not. For the good which I would, I do not: but the evil which I would not, that I practice. But if what I would not, that I do, it is no more I that do it but THE SIN *which dwelleth in me."*

"In me, that is in my flesh," means "in the lower carnal self" (Alford). "In me so far at least as my person is carnal" (Godet). "He therefore gives it to be understood that there is something in him besides the flesh, even the knowledge and admiration of goodness. There is good in the ego, but in the *understanding* only, not in the flesh which gives the active impulse."

Sarx (flesh) here, according to Lange, means not merely the body or the lusts of the body, but, also Fairchild says, "the aggregate of the desires and passions of which the bodily appetites are only the most conspicuous." "The finite *tendency* in both its immaterial and sensuous character."

The sense of this passage, then, is that THE SIN has taken possession of the sensibilities and made them, as Lange says, "a fountain of wicked action." The better self, the illuminated judgment and conscience, protests against the commission of sin; but the indwelling tyrant, with ceaseless diligence and tireless activity, rushes me on into evil conduct. It is no more *I*, the better ego, that do it, but an overmastering *I* of *"the sin* that dwelleth in me."* I am moved to do that which in conscience I would not do.

Third Cycle (verses 21-25)—

"I find then the law, that, to me who would do good, evil is present. For I delight in the law of God after the inward man: but I see a different law in my members, warring against the law of my mind, and bringing me into captivity under the law of THE SIN *which is in my members. O wretched man that I am! who shall deliver me out of the body of this death?* I THANK GOD THROUGH JESUS CHRIST OUR LORD. *So then I myself with the mind serve the law of God; but with the flesh the law of sin."*

We have the word "law" in this passage five times. In all but the second, where it refers to moral law, it means *"the governing principle"* (Godet), *"the uniform tendency"* (Daniel Steele), *"regular process, continuous action"* (Alexander Maclaren).

"I *delight* in the law of God after the inward man." That is, I regard it with complacency, and admire its precepts, "in the inmost chamber of my being." "The inward man" here is the *nous* of verses 23 and 25, the understanding and moral consciousness, which approves virtue in others. The ordinary conscience even of the natural man, as moral philosophers admit, delights in exhibitions of right and justice.

Many commentators insist that this is a picture of regeneration, because the natural man cannot have such exalted sentiments. But this is clearly a mistaken notion which has quite led them astray in interpretation. Multitudes applaud the virtues in poetic strains and exalted eloquence who are themselves anything but virtuous.

God declared that the Israelites "seek me daily and *delight* to know my ways" (Isa. 53:2), when at that very time He was threatening them with destruction for their sins. Their descendants glorified the law while they were plotting to kill Jesus. Paul himself at one time "delighted in the law of God" while he was persecuting Christians to death.

Even the heathen have delighted in the moral law while practicing sin. Ovid wrote:
"My reason this, my passion that persuades,
I see the right, and I approve it, too;
Condemn the wrong, and yet the wrong pursue."
Epictetus wrote: "He who sins does not will sin, but wishes to walk uprightly: yet it is manifest that what he *wills*, he doth not; and what he wills not, he doth." Euripides wrote: "Passion, however, is more powerful than my reason; which is the cause of the greatest evils to mortal man." It would not be difficult to name English poets who wrote beautiful Christian sentiments while their lives were unreportable. When Hodge says that an unregenerate man cannot delight in the law of God, the experience of millions contradicts his assertion. This mental delight in the law of God may be only the intellectual ideal of morality, contemplated by wicked men with admiration, but never practiced. The uniform tendency of the depraved nature (v. 23) is to override the constant sentiments and protests of the inner man and bring the poor victim into the most degrading captivity to the uniform tendency to sin and death.

After repeated struggles and endless defeats, despairing of self-betterment, the poor soul at last cries out, "O wretched man that I am, who shall deliver me from the body of this death?" Calvin comments thus: "He teaches us to ask for death as the only remedy of evil." Godet replies: "It is impossible to mistake the meaning more completely." It is not death but *Christ* who brings deliverance. *"I thank God through Jesus Christ our Lord."*

"So then I myself with the mind serve the law of God: but with the flesh the law of sin." Steele: "I myself alone, on the plane of nature, without the aid of Christ, can do no better than render a dual service, with the mind serving the law of God, by my admiration of its excellence, but with the flesh the law of sin, by such a surrender as carries my guilty personality with it." This is the summing up of the discord with the struggling sinner in his convicted law state. But God sent His Son and the Holy Spirit to give him the peace of justification and the cleansing of sanctification from *the sin* which made him all his trouble. This "double cure" "bestows a harmony divine, and this harmony peals forth in pæan in the opening of the next chapter."

CHAPTER V

DELIVERANCE BY CHRIST

"There is therefore now no condemnation to them that are in Christ Jesus. For the law of the Spirit of life in Christ Jesus made me free from the law of THE SIN *and death"* (Rom. 8:1, 2).

Paul is still relating his experience. He has described in graphic language his bitter bondage to THE SIN dwelling in him, and the failure of the law to help him, and the despair it brought. Now he tells the astonished Jews and the world what Jesus did for him. He unfolds the power and virtue of the gospel scheme. It pardons and sanctifies. The law could do neither.

Here, for the first time, he relates his present, up-to-date experience. This picture is so totally different from that described in the preceding chapter that it is absolutely impossible that they should both be the description of the same man at one and the same time. There he was a wretched captive, tugging at his chains; here he is free. There he was trying to save himself; here he is already saved by another. There he was groaning; here he is shouting happy. There it was agonizing prayer; here it is rapturous praise. There he was defeated; here he is victorious. There it was dark despair; here it is cloudless hope.

Now it is reasonable to conclude that no person could possibly be carnal, sold under *the sin,* brought into captivity to the law of *the sin* and death, and at the same time be made free from that law of *the sin* and death by the law of the Spirit of life in Christ Jesus. They are absolute, irreconcilable contradictions, mutually exclusive.

In the sixth chapter Paul exhibited sanctification and a life of holiness as provided for in the atonement, and as a blessed privilege and a solemn duty. In this chapter he reveals or exhibits it as a personal experience in his own life. He sets forth the work of the Holy Spirit as a divine principle in his life, working out in him the will of God. This admirable chapter has been called, "The chapter beginning with no *condemnation* and ending with no *separation!*" Godet reports Spener as saying: "If the Holy Scripture was a ring, and the Epistle to the Romans its precious stone, chapter 8 would be the sparkling point of the jewel." The Holy Spirit brings Christ potentially into his life, who not only justifies him, but abides in him as a new principle of death to THE SIN and life to God. The new force in his life, as the apostle bears witness, is "the Holy Spirit, by whom Christ crucified and risen reproduces Himself in the believer." Thus

Verse 1: *"There is therefore now no condemnation to them that are in Christ Jesus."*

Fully justified, pardoned, restored to the favor of God. No condemnation as the penal consequence of original and actual sin. *"In Christ Jesus"* means a vital union between Christ and His people by faith. Jesus compared it to the union between the vine and its branches. It is not legal, federal union but a living relation.

Verse 2: *"For the law of the Spirit of life in Christ Jesus made me free from the law of THE SIN and death."*

Godet affirms that verses 1-4 describe the restoration of holiness by the Holy Spirit. Sin entails death on the justified, in whom it regains the upper hand, as well as on the unjustified (8:12, 13). There is, therefore, only one way of preventing sin from causing us to perish, that is, that it perish itself.

The word "law" occurs in this second verse twice. No one can rightly interpret the seventh and eighth chapters of Romans without critically noting the sense in which the word "law" is used each time it occurs. In this verse it does not mean any *statute,* or *decree,* or legislative authoritative enactment. Dr. Maclaren points out that here it means "continuous action," "constancy of operation, uniform and fixed." Godet calls it "the controlling power imposing itself on the will." Dr. Daniel Steele, says it means *"uniform tendency."* Dr. Barnes says it means, *"the influence."* Now if we substitute any one of these phrases we shall get the meaning of the verse: "The INFLUENCE of the Spirit of life in Christ Jesus made me free from the INFLUENCE of THE SIN and the death," that is, *the moral death* that accompanies THE SIN.

This is the apostle's wonderful testimony of deliverance which he gladly proclaims to others. He believes that the controlling power of the Holy Spirit, which broke the power of THE SIN over him, can deliver others too. He knows that no mere outward means will be sufficient to emancipate their souls, for he has tried them. No mere intellectual methods will set free the passions and desires that have been captured by THE SIN PRINCIPLE. It is vain to seek deliverance from a perverted will by any revelation of moral law however emphatic. He has tried them all, and they have miserably failed. Nothing can touch the necessities of the case but the incoming Holy Spirit, as a potential indwelling Christ, whose abiding, controlling influence in us can subvert and expel the tendencies to sin. "That communicated power must impart life. Nothing short of a *Spirit of life,* quick and powerful, with an immortal sense of intense energy, will avail to meet the need."

Verse 3: *"For what the law could not do, in that it was weak through the flesh, God, sending his own Son in the likeness of sinful flesh and as an offering for sin, condemned* THE SIN *in the flesh."*

"Law" in this verse means the law of God. The moral law. This law could not justify or sanctify, as Paul knew by experience. The flesh hindered it. The flesh (*sarx*) here means *"the seat of passion and frailty,"* and then figuratively, "the carnal and rebellious principle itself" (Clarke).

"God sending his own Son in the likeness of sinful flesh." God's own Son was like Himself, holy and spiritual. He took upon Himself our nature, "the likeness of the flesh of sin," but without our sinful propensities or desires. Human nature as God made it and as Christ exhibited it is perfect. There was no *he hamartia* "THE SIN" in it. "That life of Jesus, lived in human nature," said Maclaren, "gives a new hope of the possibilities of that nature lived in us. The dream of perfect beauty 'in the flesh' has been realized. What the man Christ Jesus was, He was that we may become. In the very flesh (nature) in which the tyrant rules, Jesus shows the possibility and the loveliness of a holy life." Christ came in a real, living human nature, in a humanity subject to those same conditions of bodily existence under which we all are, and He remained, as He had ever been, "holy, harmless, undefiled, and separate from sinners."

He thus *"condemned* THE SIN *in the flesh,"* as wholly unnecessary, and no essential part of it. As Godet quotes Theophylact approvingly: "He sanctified the flesh and crowned it by condemning sin in the flesh which He had appropriated, and by showing that the flesh is not sinful in its nature." No human being has any scriptural warrant for saying that we must have sin in us so long as we remain in the body. Such a conclusion throws away the very meaning and purpose of Christ's life. Sin's hold on man is two-fold—one that it has perverted his relation to God, and the other that it has corrupted his nature. Christ, by His incarnation, provided for the pardon of the *sin* and the cleansing of the *nature*. He was "declared to be the Son of God with power according to the spirit of holiness." He baptizes with the Holy Spirit, and by the entrance of the Spirit of holiness into our nature the usurper—"THE SIN"—is driven out.

Verse 4: 'Condemned THE SIN in the flesh." God as a Judge condemned it to destruction. *"That the ordinance of the law might be fulfilled in us who walk not after the flesh but after the Spirit."* "After" means "according to" the Spirit. Clarke observes: "The design and object of the incarnation and sacrifice of Christ was to condemn sin, to have it executed and destroyed; not as some think to tolerate it or to render it subservient to the purposes of His *grace;* but to annihilate its *power, guilt,* and *being* in the soul of a believer." In the same spirit Godet says: "The condemnation of sin in Christ's life is the *means* appointed by God to effect its destruction in ours."

Alford nobly writes: "Sin is throughout the passage an *absolute* principle. It does not mean that God condemned sin by the death of Christ, for several reasons:

(1) The apostle is not speaking of the removal of *guilt,* but of the *practice* of sin. He is grounding the "no condemnation" on the new and sanctifying power of the Spirit of Christ.

(2) The context shows that the weakness of the law was its having no sanctifying power. It could arouse sin but could not *condemn* it and *cast it out*.

(3) The next verse makes the fulfilling the righteous demand of the law no matter of mere *imputation,* but of walking after the Spirit."

We must look for the meaning of the word *"condemned"* in the effects—*victory over* and *casting out* of sin (John 12:31). This is very important to the right apprehension of the whole chapter, in this part of which *not the justification* but the *sanctification* of Christians is the leading subject. Christ's victory over sin is *mine, by my union with Him and participation in His Spirit."*

Whedon says: "The righteousness of the law 'does not mean *imputed* righteousness,' nor simple innocence, but an *actual and active personal righteousness* energized by the Spirit."

Dr. Maclaren wrote: "Remember the alternative. There must be condemnation for us, or for THE SIN that dwelleth in us. There is no condemnation for them who are in Christ Jesus, because there is no condemnation for THE SIN that dwells in them. It must be slain or it will slay us. It must be cast out or it will cast us out from God. It must be separated from us, or it will separate us from Him. We need not be condemned, but if it be not condemned, then we shall be."

CHAPTER VI

DEATH, OR GLORY
(Romans 8:5-14)

"For they that are after the flesh do mind the things of the flesh: but they that are after the Spirit, the things of the Spirit. For the mind of the flesh is death, but the mind of the Spirit is life and peace" (Rom. 8:5, 6).

On the previous section (verses 1-4) Lange tells us: "Christ, by becoming man in the flesh, and yet having a sinless, fleshly nature, so maintained this sinlessness and holiness . . . that He made it manifest:

(1) That sin does not belong to the flesh in itself, but is inherent in it as a foreign, unnatural, condemnable, *separable, alienable* element:

(2) That sin in the flesh is condemned and rejected in its carnal appearance;

(3) That sin in the flesh should be separated from the entire human nature by means of the Spirit proceeding from Christ."

We say, Amen! That is precisely what we are trying to teach.

Now the verses before us tell why God wishes us to be rid of this carnal principle. "For those who are under the power of the carnal, rebellious principle," "think of, care for," "relish," "strive after" "the things of the flesh," having no relish for spiritual and eternal things; but they that are AFTER THE SPIRIT, the things of the Spirit." "After" means "in accordance with," "in harmony with," the Spirit. Meyer says, " 'After the Spirit' designates only the *sanctifying Divine principle itself,* and not the human spirit." We must choose between these two ruling

principles. There is no avoiding it. And in the next verse
the apostle urges us by the most awful motives that can
be named to a right choice.

*"For the mind of the flesh is death: but the mind of
the Spirit is life and peace."*

To live under the influence of the carnal mind—the
depraved tendencies of our fallen nature—and to yield
to them is to be headed for destruction, and to be liable
any hour to be numbered among the damned. Yea, it is
already moral death. But he who has the mind of the
Spirit has already the life and peace of God in his soul,
and has heaven full in view. And he has "peace," the soul
of life. "Peace with God is connection with the source of
life; peace with oneself, a blessed sense of life; peace
with the government of God and His world, an infinitely
richer life" (Lange). Sanctified people need nobody's
pity, especially the pity of carnal worldlings. They already have heaven begun in their hearts.

In the next verse the apostle explains why *the indwelling sin* is so dangerous.

Verse 7: *"Because the mind of the flesh is enmity
against God, for it is not subject to the law of God, neither indeed can it be."*

The word for "enmity" means "a principle or state of
enmity"—the essence of hatred. "Because it is a carnal
mind, and relishes earthly and sinful things, and lives in
opposition to the pure and holy law of God, therefore it
is *enmity* against God; it is irreconcilable and implacable
hatred. *"It is not subject to the law of God."* It will come
under no obedience, for it is *sin* and the very principle of
rebellion; and it cannot be subject, or subjected for it is
essential to the sin principle to show itself in rebellion;
and when it ceases to *rebel*, it ceases to be sin." It dies.

So Clarke observes: "From this we learn that the design of God in the economy of the gospel is not to *weaken, curtail,* or lay the carnal principle in *bonds* (repress), but to destroy it. As it is not subject, and cannot be subject to the law of God, it must be *destroyed,* else it will continue to rebel against God. It cannot be mended or rendered less offensive in its nature, even by the operations of God. It is ever sin, and sin is ever enmity; and enmity, wherever it has opportunity, will invariably show itself in acts of hostility and rebellion against God."

Verse 8: *"And they that are in the flesh cannot please God."*

This word "flesh" cannot mean *"body"* here. Enoch dwelt in the body: "And before his translation he had this witness borne to him that he had been well-pleasing to God." Jesus dwelt in a body; and the Father said: "This is my beloved Son, in whom I am well pleased." No; *"in the flesh,"* like the phrase "after the flesh," means to be in subjection to *this sin principle,* which perverts and deranges all our sensibilities, prompting obedience to them rather than obedience to right reason, illuminated by the Holy Spirit. *"Cannot please God."* That settles it. This principle of sin that infests our being must be condemned and executed, so that we may be wholly loyal and well-pleasing to God.

People may talk about taming, and subduing, and repressing, baptizing into respectability this inbred sin, this child of the devil, all they like. No such idea is scriptural. It is not to be *"repressed,"* nor *suppressed,* nor *oppressed,* but *expressed* out of our being. The Bible terms are "take away," "purge away," "destroy," "consume by fire," "cleanse from," "eliminate," "mortify," or "kill." And the real blood-bought, truly saved children of God, who really love Him, will be so anxious to please Him that they will earnestly plead for the sin-consuming, cleansing baptism with the Holy Spirit and fire to burn out this sinful dross from their hearts, and make them wholly pleasing to God.

Verse 9: *"But ye are not in the flesh but in the Spirit, if so be that the Spirit of God dwelleth in you."*

The Spirit sustains three relations to believers: *"para," with* us, *"en," in* us, and *"epi," upon* us. *He* was *with* the disciples before the crucifixion (John 14:17). Jesus then promised that He should be *in* them, and it was fulfilled at Pentecost. Also He was *upon* them for *power* (Acts 1:8). Here, then, the apostle sets forth the experience of sanctification. *Eiper,* "provided that" if only "the Spirit of God dwelleth in you." The flesh, the sinful principle, possesses men, ruling sinners and tormenting unsanctified believers, opposing everything good within them. But Jesus proposes to cleanse the temple, and make man again "a habitation of God through the Spirit." When Jesus baptizes with the Holy Spirit for cleansing, He comes in and puts out *the sinful principle,* His enemy and ours, and fills the vacated nature with Himself, to abide in us for ever. This is absolutely necessary to our present peace and our final salvation.

Verse 9: *"But if any man hath not the Spirit of Christ, he is none of his."*

If any man has not his Holy Spirit in some degree of power, either *with* him or *in* him, to subdue or put out this sin-principle, he is none of His. Lange: "The apostle does not regard a merely external belonging to Christ as of any value. Where the Christianity of the inward life is extinct, there the Christianity of the whole man is extinct."

Verse 10: *"And if Christ is in you, the body is dead because of sin: but the spirit is life because of righteousness."*

Verse 11: *"But if the Spirit of him that raised up Jesus from the dead dwelleth in you, he that raised up Christ Jesus from the dead shall quicken also your mortal bodies through his Spirit that dwelleth in you."*

Alford says: "The righteousness of verse 10 is not imputed righteousness, but the implanted righteousness of the sanctification of the Spirit." The meaning of this passage seems to be this, as most in harmony with the context. Sin brought the death-principle upon the race, and the sentence of death must be fulfilled on every human being until the judgment. No doubt this spiritual life of sanctification will not prevent our bodies from dying; but it is the earnest of its participation in the glorious resurrection of Christ. He who here receives the Spirit of Christ in sanctifying fullness, and continues to live a life of obedience to the divine will, shall have a glorious resurrection to life eternal.

Sanctification removes the artificial and abnormal appetites from the body, and leaves the necessary and innocent natural appetites in a normal degree of strength, to be controlled by the sanctified reason. But still, death being a judgment on humanity, bearing on the *species* as such, the body must die, even though sanctified. Godet says: " '*dead*' means irrevocably smitten with death." We mention in passing that Chrysostom, Grotius, and others explain the term "dead" as *"dead unto sin."* This, if correct, would make the doctrine of sanctification all the stronger. The indwelling Spirit purifies the entire man, even the body, and restores all to God.

Verses 12 and 13: *"So then, brethren, we are debtors, not to the flesh to live after the flesh: for if ye live after the flesh, ye must die: but if by the Spirit ye mortify the deeds of the body, ye shall live."*

"The natural man," Hoffman observes, "imagines that he owes it to his flesh to satisfy it." "The flesh here," says Whedon and Miley, "is a depravity not confined to the body, but including the entire tendency to sin." Barnes says, *"Sarx* (flesh) here is the corrupt propensities and passions." "The apostle then says that we do not owe these corrupt propensities and passions gratification. We are not bound to indulge them, because the end is death and ruin (in the fullest sense of eternal ruin). *"But if ye mortify the deeds of the body ye shall live"* (life eternal). Lange says: "Mortify means to exhaust or abnegate to the very root." Barnes says it means "To put to death, destroy." " 'Deeds of the body' consist in the *predominance* of *illegal impulses"* (Lange). "The corrupt inclinations and passions are called the deeds of *the body* because they are supposed to have their origin in the fleshly appetites" (Barnes). . . . "Either your sins and evil propensities must die, or you must. If they are suffered to live you will die. If they are put to death, you will be saved. No man can be saved in his sins."

Verse 14: *"For as many as are led by the Spirit of God, these are the sons of God."*

"This," says Lange, "gives the reason why they shall live." By the indwelling, sanctifying Spirit the propensities of the carnal nature are mortified, and they are continually led in the way of holiness, and so are the sons of God. "One evidence of piety is a willingness to yield to that influence and submit to the Spirit. One decided evidence of the want of piety is an unwillingness to submit to that influence, but where the Holy Spirit is grieved and resisted" (Barnes). The influence of the Spirit, if followed, would lead every man into the experience of sanctification, and finally to heaven. But when neglected, rejected, or despised, man, driven on by his own carnality, makes his final home in hell.

Thus closes this tremendous argument. It has proved that what the law could not do the Gospel, revealing Christ and the Infinite Spirit of God, accomplishes, *viz.*, the sanctification of the soul, the destruction of the depraved tendencies of our nature, and the recovery in man of the image of God.

Then follow all the other blessings named in this wonderful chapter, as the glorious day follows the coming of the morning sun. We only have time to name them: *"The witness of the Spirit."* The conscious sonship of God, the joint heirship with Christ, the victory over suffering, the intercession of the Spirit, the shaping of all the providences of God in our favor, till we become conquerors, and more than conquerors, through Him that loved us. They all follow the incoming of the sanctifying Spirit like a trail of shining angels following their Leader—Christ. The sanctified soul, amazed at the prodigal wealth of its possessions of salvation, breaks out with the apostle in his "hymn of assurance"—"I am persuaded that neither death, nor life, nor angels, nor principalities, nor things present, nor things to come, nor powers, nor height, nor depth, nor any other creature, shall be able to separate us from the love of God, which is in Christ Jesus our Lord." And so the singing pilgrim passes on in "the way of holiness" till he is lost in view, mounting up with swift feet the shining steps that lead to the Celestial City.

CHAPTER VII

HOLY AND ACCEPTABLE TO GOD

"I beseech you therefore, brethren, by the mercies of God, to present your bodies a living sacrifice, holy, acceptable to God, which is your reasonable service. And be not fashioned according to this world: but be ye transformed by the renewing of your mind, that ye may prove what is the good and acceptable and perfect will of God" (Rom. 12:1, 2).

The exposition of Christian doctrine in this Epistle closes with the eleventh chapter in a doxology of praise. The apostle has built with massive logic a temple of faith which has stood the assaults of Christ's foes through all the centuries, and has ever been the peaceful home of devout souls. "In chapters 1-4 he has shown that, in spite of the awful wickedness of men, they could be justified by faith; and they can also be sanctified in Christ by the communication of the Spirit (5-8); and it is precisely the refusal to follow this way which has drawn down on Israel their rejection (9-11)" (Godet).

Now he passes to the practical application of the doctrines. "I beseech you therefore brethren, by the mercies of God." "Therefore" refers to the entire argument of the preceding eleven chapters—God's plan of full salvation. It leads to the practical appeal. Thus Christian living is inseparably connected with Christian believing. And, notice further, it is an appeal to *Christians* to rise in their experience to *the second blessing.* He wrote the Epistle to people "beloved of God, called to be saints."

He calls them "brethren," and appeals to them "by the mercies of God," which they had experienced in their hearts, to give themselves anew to God for the *blessing of sanctification.*

I. Let us consider the required duty.

"To present your bodies a living sacrifice." It is a duty urged upon Christians in sacrificial language with which the Jews were perfectly familiar. The verb "to present" is in the aorist tense meaning "to present yourself once for all," to be the Lord's for time and eternity. There is a tacit contrast drawn between the old sacrificial ritual and the true Christian sacrifice and service. The analogy suggests the meaning of the text, and makes the teaching clear.

1. THE OLD ISRAELITES WERE REQUIRED TO BRING SACRIFICES, BUT ALWAYS SOMETHING WITHIN THE MEANS OF THE WORSHIPER. The rich man might bring a wedge of gold as an offering. He might bring bullocks to the altar, or a heifer. A poorer man might bring a lamb. A family very poor would be accepted if they brought a dove, or, by fasting for one meal, a handful of fine flour. It was to be something of their *own* for God. God asks believers who would be sanctified "to present their bodies"—a gift certainly within the power of each to give.

"Now Paul," says Dr. Maclaren, "was not such a superficial moralist as to begin at the wrong end, and talk about the surrender of the outward life unless as the result of the prior surrender of the inward. For a priest needs to be consecrated before he can offer, and we in our innermost wills, in the depths of our nature, must be surrendered and set apart to God ere our outward self can be laid on the altar. So there must first be internal surrender. 'Yield yourselves unto God, and your bodies as instruments of righteousness unto him.' "

Our bodies and souls are now joined. He cannot get them unless our souls who inhabit them give consent. So, as the ultimate fact, it means that God wants our whole selves. Nothing else will answer but a complete, all-including sacrifice.

What a field for consecration! The eye so absolutely given to God that it shall not be allowed to look upon the evil that is calculated to awake wrong desires in the heart; "that looks with complacency on things pure, and turns from the impure as if a hot iron had been thrust into its pupil"; the ear so devoted that it consents to hear only what its Lord would have it hear; the lips so consecrated that they shall speak for God; the appetites to be gratified only as the good of being demands; the hands to be engaged only in the ministry of love, and the feet to walk only in the paths of righteousness, and be swift and beautiful for God; the whole to be a temple of the Holy Ghost, in which the Lord of life is ever on the throne!

2. WHEN WE HAVE THUS GIVEN OURSELVES TO GOD WE ARE OUR OWN NO LONGER. When the Israelite brought an offering he surrendered all claim to it. So with the Christian consecrating for this blessing. He surrenders all claim to himself. Intellect, will, affections, desires, possessions, influence—all are God's, and are never again to be taken from the altar.

3. THIS IS A "LIVING SACRIFICE." The ancient lamb gave up its life to be a sacrifice; but we keep ours. The mind goes out as ever before on excursions of thought. The will still sits upon the throne as the arbiter of des-

tiny. But it is all for God. He now inhabits the sensibilities to thrill the soul with such emotions as please Him. We are still our own conscious selves, minus indwelling sin which the Spirit removes, plus the Divine Being ruling within.

Solemn fact! While our bodies are primarily subject to ourselves, yet we are so made that another spirit may dwell within us—the spirit of the world, the spirit of the age, the spirit of Satan, or the Spirit of God. Oh, that it may not be the spirit of darkness transformed into an angel of light, but the sanctifying Spirit of God transfiguring me into His likeness!

II. The sacrifice is to be holy.

You may say, "Ah, how can I, so imperfect and unworthy and unlike God, ever give such an offering to Him?" Return to the figure of the text. The old Israelite might have said, "My cattle are all alike in disposition. None of them is particularly holy." But one is caught and brought to the altar, and lo! as it touches the altar "it is made holy." "The altar sanctifieth the gift." So it is with us. If we wait until we are holy before we present ourselves to God we will never make the gift. But it is not that better somebody of the future whom God wants; it is *you*, as you are, with all your unworthiness, but hating sin and longing to be sanctified. Christ is your High Priest. He, too, is your altar. Bring yourself to Him and He will make you holy.

III. "Acceptable to God."

Strange that it should be! But God is not a hard Master. He looks down in pity upon His weary, sin-sick child, seeking a perfect recovery, and says, "Poor thing!

he has done his best; she hath done what she could, an angel could do no more." And it is accepted according to that a man hath. Somehow, in some way, God will let you know that you are accepted. The old priest entered the holy of holies with the blood, and came out alive—the proof that his sacrifice had been accepted. The smoking furnace and burning lamp satisfied Abraham's heart. In Elijah's case the fire fell. Jesus said, "I will manifest myself unto him," and that is enough for you. *How,* does not matter. Leave your offering with Jesus, content until He lets you know it is accepted. "Cast not away, therefore, your confidence, which hath great recompense of reward; for ye have need of patience, that, after ye have done the will of God, ye might receive the promise."

IV. It is a "reasonable service."

Is sanctification too much? Jesus prayed for it, and died for it, and it is His will. Has not God such a claim upon us? Can we give the Infinite Christ too much who gave His all for us? Creator! Preserver! Redeemer! Oh, let me give myself entirely to Him, to show forth His praise.

Many are afraid of losing something. Yes, you will lose ever so much—corruption, the damning sin! the inward strife! the constant defeats! Your old companions may fall away as the withes fell from the limbs of the aroused Samson. But oh! the gain!—purity, peace, victory, Godlikeness of character, the indwelling of the keeping Spirit, heaven! What a gain for what a loss!

V. "Be not conformed to the WORLD."

An English bishop says, "The world is human society organizing itself apart from God." It means those fashions, maxims, customs, principles of action, sentiments, aims and feelings which imperiously rule unregenerate lives. All these taken together constitute that hostile world which crucified Christ and is still in deadly opposition to the kingdom of God. "If any man love the world, the love of the Father is not in him."

But that is the characteristic weakness of the church of our time. The great bulk of its membership is "in torpid conformity with the world." It is swayed by the world's ambitions, delighted by the world's pleasures, intoxicated by the world's applause, ruled by the world's customs and fashions and laws. They measure themselves by the world's standards, and try to slake the thirst of their souls from the world's fountain of pleasures. God knows it. Angels know it. Devils know it. Unregenerate men know it, and unanimously vote that such mawkish piety is only detestable cant and hypocrisy. Well does God call upon us to get a blessing and a kind of salvation that will spoil us for "the world."

VI. "Be transformed"—"transfigured."

The same Greek word describes Jesus' transfiguration. Let a person get this blessing which the apostle is urging upon Christians, and they will be transfigured sure enough. The lines of care and impatience and restlessness will be smoothed out. The look of spiritual hunger will disappear. A new shine will come into the countenance and a new light into the eye. The look of heavenly peace and rest will transfigure the face. "Another worldliness" will appear in the life. The ambitions, temper, plans, purposes, and aims of life will all be metamorphosed into the image of Christ. One smile from Him will be more highly prized than the approbation of the world for ever.

Such a Christian will *know* by a blessed personal experience, and "prove what is the good and acceptable and perfect will of God." "This is the will of God, even your sanctification . . . for God hath called you into sanctification" (1 Thess. 4:3, 7). Few Christians, compared with the great number of professors of religion, have any conception of what Christ's salvation might do for them. The very word "sanctification" means nothing to them. But God wants them to know and *prove by experience* how sweet and blessed is His perfect will concerning us.

VII. Now the exhortation, "I BESEECH YOU."

How anxious the great apostle must have been that his fellow-Christians should get rid of "THE SIN" dwelling in them which had been such a bane to his own life! He knew the weakness it induced, the moral defeats it caused, the temptations it fostered, the sins it begot, the peace it destroyed. So with a tenderness of devotion, with a passionate earnestness he writes, "I BESEECH YOU." Take the blessing that will make you *"holy, acceptable,"* wholly pleasing to God, and prepared to dwell in His presence. The new Queen Mary of England has let it be known that ladies dressed in a certain mode may not come into her court. So has decided the Infinite King. We must be "holy" to be acceptable to Him. "The sanctification without which no man shall see the Lord."

God is ready. Jesus died for it. He calls you to make the sacrifice that He may sanctify you. "NOW," while you read these lines, "is the acceptable time." Say now,

"A body hast Thou prepared for me." "I give it Thee O God." "Lo, I come to do Thy will."

The lamb had to be taken to the temple. But God would make you His sanctified temple. Now, as you are, and where you are consent, make the sacrifice, and trust God to accept it and make you the fit temple of the Holy Ghost. Then will follow the life described in this twelfth chapter of Romans, which, with the Sermon on the Mount and the thirteenth of 1 Corinthians, is the finest picture of a holy life in the entire Word of God.

CHAPTER VIII

"SANCTIFIED BY THE HOLY GHOST"

"That I should be a minister of Christ Jesus unto the Gentiles, ministering the gospel of God, that the offering up of the Gentiles might be made acceptable, BEING SANCTIFIED BY THE HOLY SPIRIT" (Rom. 15:16).

The apostle thought of the grace of God that made him a minister to the Gentiles. His parish was the Gentile world. His mind kindled at the thought. By a grand figure the apostle makes himself a priest under Christ to perform a sacrifice in which the offering to God is the Gentile nations. His imagination is on fire as he seems to himself to be approaching the Gentile world through Christ to the living God. The victim upon the Jewish altar was fitted for the offering by salt, or oil, or frankincense. But these Gentiles were to be made acceptable to God by *"being sanctified by the Holy Ghost."* Thus the truth of Rom. 12:1 is repeated here, only more definitely, viz., *we must be sanctified to be wholly acceptable to God.* Consider then,

I. The Spirit promised.

God spake by the mouth of Joel: "And it shall come to pass in the last days, saith God, I will pour forth of my Spirit upon all flesh. . . . Yea, and on my servants and on my handmaidens in those days will I pour forth of my Spirit." By Isaiah He said: "I will pour water upon him that is thirsty. . . . I will pour my Spirit" (Isa. 44:3). By Ezekiel He said: "I will sprinkle clean water [type of the Spirit] upon you, and ye shall be clean. . . .

And I will put my Spirit within you, and cause you to walk in my statutes. . . . And I will save you from all your uncleanness" (Ezek. 36:25, 27, 29). Through the mouth of John the Baptist He said: "I indeed baptize you with water unto repentance, but he that cometh after me is mightier than I, whose shoes I am not worthy to bear; he shall baptize you with the Holy Spirit and with fire."

Then came Jesus repeating and amplifying all the promises about the pouring out of the Spirit and fire, and His last message was: "Wait for the promise of the Father, which ye heard from me: for John indeed baptized with water, but ye shall be baptized with the Holy Spirit not many days hence."

II. We are encouraged to pray for this Holy Spirit.

After promising the pouring out of the Spirit in cleansing power through Ezekiel, God said, "For this, moreover, will I be inquired of by the house of Israel to do it for them." Jesus said, "If ye, then, being evil, know how to give good gifts unto your children, how much more shall your heavenly Father give the Holy Spirit to them that ask him?" And His parting word was, "Tarry ye in Jerusalem until ye be endued with power from on high." "Ye shall have power after that the Holy Spirit is come upon you" (Luke 24:49; Acts 1:8). They went back to Jerusalem to that prayer-chamber, and "These all with one accord continued steadfastly in prayer." This marvelous blessing that has such amazing effects upon the lives of men is no accident. It was promised by the prophets and by Jesus. How to get it was made known, and it is always prayed down from the skies.

III. The Spirit was poured out.

The blessed promises were fulfilled. The earnest prayers were answered. Pentecost came. The condition being fulfilled, the same blessing was bestowed elsewhere, and at other times, even through all the ages. Peter and John went down to Samaria to pray for the young converts of Samaria "that they might receive the Holy Spirit." The apostles felt that it was supremely important that the converts shall receive the second blessing and be sanctified, Spirit-filled Christians. "And they received the Holy Spirit" (Acts 8:15, 17).

There were some young converts at Cæsarea—Cornelius and his household. They were, especially Cornelius, "righteous," "one that feared God," "a devout man," one who "prayed to God always," "worked righteousness, and was accepted of God" (Acts 10:2, 22, 30, 31, 35). Yet God was so exceedingly anxious that these Christians should receive the sanctifying Spirit, that He sent an angel to Cornelius and a vision to Peter to get them together, that these converts might receive the Holy Spirit.

There was a little church in Ephesus. Paul, in his travels, went there, and in his first service he asked, "Did you receive the Holy Spirit when ye believed?" They answered, "Nay, we did not so much as hear whether the Holy Spirit was given." Multitudes of congregations would be obliged to confess the same today. They are never urged by their pastors to seek the baptism with the Holy Spirit for heart-cleansing and the enduement of power. But this matchless blessing was not for the people of any age or place. Peter said at Pentecost, "Ye shall receive the gift of the Holy Spirit; for the promise is to you and to your children, and to all that are afar off, even as many as the Lord our God shall call unto him" (Acts 2:38, 39). Every one that has a call to be a Christian at all is called to be a *sanctified Christian,* filled with the Holy Spirit. Through all the centuries, even to our day, God has gladly bestowed the blessing upon all willing, consecrated, and believing hearts.

IV. Notice the purpose of the blessing.

If our discussion of Romans 5-8 has not been unpardonably lacking in clearness, it has made plain to every reader that *"the sin"* dwelling in us is the prolific fountain of all moral evil in our life. We have seen how it was personified as the "warring queen," "the old man," "the body of sin," the cruel "slave-master," the "law of sin," the "murderer." We have seen that it was called the very essence of "enmity against God" that never can be tamed or brought into subjection, or be reconciled with anything good.

Moreover, we have seen again and again in the sixth chapter that *"the sin,"* this "old man" of corruption, this "body of death," this cruel master, may be "crucified" and "destroyed," so that we are *"made free from sin."* In the eighth chapter we were told how it is done. The great apostle, giving his experience, said, "The Spirit made free" (8:2). And this idea is repeated over and over again through a dozen verses. Now, that is exactly what the text means: "Being sanctified by the Holy Spirit." Peter, years afterward, describing the blessing that came to Cornelius and his friends, said: "And God, who knoweth the hearts, bare them witness, giving them the Holy Spirit, . . . *cleansing their hearts by faith."* The eminent theologian, Dr. Daniel Steele says: "Sanctification is the act of God's grace removing impurity **existing** in the nature of one already born of the Spirit." The conquering Holy Ghost. Law, philosophy, self-culture, Standard Dictionary defines sanctification: "Specifically in theology, the gracious work of the Spirit whereby the believer is freed from sin and exalted to holiness of heart and life."

So if any soul wishes to be freed from the "carnal mind," "*the sin*" that was born in him and "dwells" in him, prompting him to every kind of evil and iniquity, the dictionary and our text and the eighth chapter of Romans tells him just how to receive the blessing. Let him persistently seek the baptism with the Holy Spirit. He can come into the life with a fiery, sin-consuming energy that will utterly burn up the chaff and dross of the nature, and leave the heart clean to be the temple of the indwelling Spirit.

This is the blessing that brings victory to the daily life. It is the vile *sin-principle* inside the heart that is the source of the ever-recurring moral defeats of men. The over-boiling and ebullitions, the rasping impatience, the hot words that stab like daggers the hearts we love, the incessant yielding to habits we hate and would be rid of, the cooling off of devotion to God, the chill of ardor in spiritual service, the apathy and indifference and deadness to divine things, the lukewarmness of heart and loss of first love, and a thousand other symptoms of waning piety—they all come from "*the sin*" discussed in this Epistle to the Romans. The moral law cannot remove it. The inner conflict in the soul between holy aspirations and evil propensities, between good resolutions and evil desires, can never cease, and the civil war can never end, until this evil principle is "destroyed." It can be utterly cast out and eliminated from the life. But only one power ever revealed to man can do it—that is, the cleansing, all-agonizing effort, tears, prayer, have all been tried, and all have ignominiously failed. But the Omnipotent God coming into the soul, the sanctifying, sin-consuming, carnality-slaying Holy Spirit coming into the citadel of our nature, can bind the strong man, kill him, and cast him out. Then for the first time in the experience, the conflict will be over. "The peace of God that passeth all understanding shall keep your hearts and minds through Christ Jesus."

This is what the Spirit was given for. A million ages ago, "God chose you from the beginning unto salvation in sanctification of the Spirit" (2. Thess. 2:13). He planned this world to be the home of sanctified Christians. To doubt the possibility of such an experience is to misread and misinterpret and doubt the unchangeable truth of the holy God.

V. This coming of the Spirit in sanctifying power is conditioned on our faith.

We are "sanctified *by faith* that is in me" (Acts 26:18). "That we might receive the promise of the Spirit *through faith*" (Gal. 3:14). "Giving them the Holy Ghost . . . cleansing their hearts *by faith*" (Acts 15:8, 9).

But we cannot believe for this blessing till we have first complied with other conditions. There must be absolute surrender to obey God about everything (Acts 5:32). There must be absolute consecration of yourself to God. "Present yourselves unto God" (Rom. 6:13). Then pray for the blessing in faith: "He giveth the Holy Spirit to them that ask him" (Luke 11:13). Dr. A. J. Gordon, the noble, sanctified Baptist preacher of Boston, said: "It seems clear from the Scriptures that it is still *the duty and privilege of believers to receive the Holy Spirit by a conscious, definite act of* APPROPRIATING FAITH, *just as they receive Jesus Christ. For it is as sinners that we accept Christ for our justification, but it is as sons, we accept the Spirit for our sanctification.*"